ONE IN THE TRUTH?

One in the Truth?

The cancer of division in the Evangelical church

ROBERT AMESS

KINGSWAY PUBLICATIONS
EASTBOURNE

Unless otherwise indicated, biblical quotations are from
the Holy Bible: New International Version, copyright © International
Bible Society, 1973, 1978, 1984.

Front cover design by Vic Mitchell

British Library Cataloguing in Publication Data

Amess, Robert
    One in the truth.
    1. Christian union
    I. Title
    262'.72   BX8.2

    ISBN 0–86065–439–7

Printed in Great Britain for
KINGSWAY PUBLICATIONS LTD
Lottbridge Drove, Eastbourne, E. Sussex BN23 6NT by
Richard Clay Ltd, Bungay, Suffolk.
Typeset by Watermark, Hampermill Cottage, Watford, WD1 4PL

Contents

Foreword

When Robert Amess was called to be the Minister of the historic Duke Street Baptist Church, Richmond, many of us rejoiced but few were surprised. This was not only because of his unique preaching gift or his robust Evangelical position, but because of his catholic spirit and moderate stand on controversial issues. It was right therefore that he should be invited to write a book on the subject of Evangelical unity.

The view put forward in this book is as balanced as one could hope for. This alas may bring the writer, who is by nature non-controversial, into heated controversy. I hope this will not be the case, however, and I express to the reader my own prayer that healing will follow rather than endless debates. I do believe that a book like this will only help.

His plea for unity is not about compromise but holding our distinctives in love. You will detect early on a compassionate understanding of those with whom he may not be in total agreement. I suspect that his central argument will not always please those in the more extreme wings of Evangelicalism, and yet he comes as it were on bended knee to appeal to them.

I have been challenged in certain areas when I noticed that

the author has been more magnanimous than I myself would have been. Every church leader should read this. Although Mr Amess is a Baptist and writes from a reformed position, let no one, whether non-conformist or Anglican, suppose it is not relevant for those who may not share his own ecclesiological and soteriological views. This is precisely why everybody should look at this book more carefully.

What follows is truly summarised by the Puritan Richard Baxter (1615–91):

> In things essential – unity;
> In things doubtful – liberty;
> In all things – charity.

R.T. Kendall

Introduction

The story is told of a soldier in the American Civil War who, wishing to preserve his life, wore a uniform of light blue shirt and dark blue trousers. Inevitably he was shot at by both sides. That is what will happen to me because of this book. It will please none and antagonise many. People who walk in the middle of the road must expect to be knocked down.

Those with an all-embracing ecclesiology will probably find this book separatistic, and the separatists will say I am compromising. But I firmly believe that this is the position I must maintain before God, therefore I have no alternative but to face the consequences before men, even as I must one day give an account before God. Throughout my ministry, particularly during the seven years in Ipswich, I have tried to practise what I preach in regard to Evangelical unity, and the undeniable blessing of God has been upon us. By nothing more than the regular, systematic preaching of the word of God, literally hundreds have come week by week to listen. As the word preached has been applied in our relationships with other Evangelical churches in the area, love, trust and harmony have been built up to the glory of God. For that I shall be eternally grateful.

In my new responsibility as the Minister of Duke Street Baptist Church in Richmond, West London, it is my earnest prayer that what God has seen fit to bless graciously in the past he may yet see fit to bless again.

1

All One in Christ Jesus?

Why should a book on Evangelical unity be regarded as controversial? I think it is partly because separation is the climate of the day. Books are written, conferences convened and papers discussed whose end result is not to strengthen the ties that bind us together but to pull us ever further apart. Despite the unequivocal teaching of Holy Scripture, despite the great high priestly prayer of the Saviour, despite the fact that every biblical metaphor for the church implies its basic unity, on every hand fragmentation is taking place.

Evangelicalism today is not marked by mutual trust and affection but rather distrust, recrimination and animosity. 'Perfect love drives out fear' (1 Jn 4:18), but I have discovered that for many fear is the order of the day. Fear of their constituency and fear of its leaders. Fear of what men might say. Fear of being labelled 'compromising' by some and 'uncommitted' by others. The more prevalent question seems to be not 'What does the Bible say?' but 'What will be my position if I seek to implement it?'

Men have confessed to me that their dread of discovering certain areas of fellowship and ministry closed to them has weighed upon them more heavily than their responsibility before God and his written word. Today many have refused to be disciples of men but rather of the Saviour, and are now desperately lonely. It is indicative of the problem that when I was invited to write this book, my first thought was not the joy of the opportunity and challenge to put into print the matter that I have been thinking about for some time, but the recrimination that would inevitably follow. Nevertheless, in the present climate of today, when the winds of division blow strong and cold, someone somewhere must stand up and be counted.

There are about one million Evangelical Christians in Britain today. A paltry number, under 2% of the population. But the desperate need of our nation at this time has not driven us together. The word 'evangelical' suggests glad tidings, good news, yet whole tracts of the country and large segments of the population are ignorant of the love of God revealed in Christ. Our energies are dissipated and morale reduced by in-fighting and recrimination. Rather than standing together in proclamation, rather than harnessing our energies for the glory of God and our mutual encouragement, the body of Christ is in danger of being torn limb from limb. The trumpet sounds with a cracked voice. In some areas truth is sacrificed, and in other areas truth is invoked to deny the essential truth of the unity of all believers. We might pay lip service to the words, 'All one in Christ Jesus' (Gal 3:28), but it goes no further.

There is a cancer in Evangelicalism today that is spreading so quickly that unless painful surgery takes place, God will give his glory to another. Unless those of us who name the name of Christ submit to the knife of God's word, however painful, 'Ichabod' will be written over the whole. The sovereign purpose of God will not be thwarted. He will accomplish his will either with us, apart from us or even against us. He will not use people who consider as unclean those whom he is blessing. Nor is our cry of 'Lord! Lord!' any guarantee of the Almighty's recognition.

The true church has many marks and we will discuss them

later. But for the moment the Scripture says of its members, 'By their fruit you will recognise them' (Mt 7:20). They will be members of the one vine (Jn 15:1–8), and will bear much fruit. The fruit of the Spirit is well known (Gal 5:22–23), but could it honestly be said that love, joy, peace, patience, kindness, goodness, faithfulness, gentleness and self-control are the marks of modern Evangelicalism that come most readily to mind? God has spoken, his word is plain, and unless we repent of our wicked ways his judgement will come upon us.

This problem is not restricted to the British church. On a recent visit to the USA I found the situation to be very similar. The same fears were expressed, the same names quoted, the same journals read. There was the same breaking up of the body of Christ. At one conference I attended, which itself had separated from another, the divisions were so deep, so painful and apparently intractable that its very continuance had come under question. Yet the people were warm-hearted and hospitable, eagerly seeking the mind and will of God. What had gone wrong?

We live in an age of Evangelical division. Who is responsible? Certainly we live in a complex time, certainly we are subject to pressures that were largely unknown to our forebears, certainly there are issues on which any man of integrity must take his stand, but at the end of the day we are forced to confess that an enemy has done this. It has been the devil's work.

There is a love of controversy within Evangelicalism today, a contentious spirit, a party mentality that has never been so prevalent before. Paul describes the marks of true love in 1 Corinthians 13. We know them well. But there is little patience among us, much of what is said is not kind, jealousy of another man's ministry is rife, boasting is the order of the day, and our arrogance is frightening. Yet Christian love is not rude, and never self-seeking. It does not seek to establish its own position or further its own end. Neither

13

is it easily angered, and it certainly keeps no record of wrongs. If the truth were not so heartbreakingly sad it would be almost funny. Love always protects, always trusts, always hopes, always perseveres – but not, it appears, among many Evangelical Christians. This paraphrase of 1 Corinthians 13 makes the point:

> Though in declaring Christ to the sinner
> I may all men surpass,
> If love in passion seal not the message
> I'm naught but sounding brass.

I'm going to use here five negative statements to describe what I am seeking to do in this book. The first should be obvious by now.

This book is not about separation but Evangelical unity

It will examine some of the pressures and problems facing Evangelical Christians today which tend to pull them apart. The undoubted difficulties will be faced, and intractable heartaches acknowledged. I am not so naïve as to think for a moment that the balm for the healing of the body of Christ will be discovered within these pages. The ever-widening charismatic/non-charismatic divide, the gulf between Evangelicals within the 'mixed denominations' and those outside, the continuing Reformed/non-Reformed polarisation cannot be bridged by one book or one mind. In the understanding of truth there are certain areas where anyone of integrity must stand, and in so doing stand apart. Yet arms of love can and must be stretched out. We must try to understand what others are saying and thinking. It is not necessarily our various positions but rather our attitudes that are offensive to God. I plead that the matters discussed in this book should be graciously considered and debated among us.

The church is a body of people, a family. We must say to one another, whatever the cost, 'If you are a son or daughter of God then you are a brother or sister of mine and must be treated as such.' As in all families there will be tensions, even disagreements, but the family must not be broken apart. If the Lord Jesus Christ is the Saviour of another as he is of me, then I will not, dare not, cannot dismiss or ignore the one he loves, whom he has redeemed by his blood. To do so is to argue with God and to repudiate his sovereign work.

In the early days of the Brethren movement, A.N. Groves, a man of great faith, was concerned about the trends in Plymouth and had an almost prophetic understanding of where the emphasis of J.N. Darby would lead. That he was right is a matter of history. That the spirit of Darby still lives is disturbingly obvious. What Groves wrote, then, has to be heard again. It is the very essence of all I am endeavouring to say. He speaks in a letter first of fellowship with individuals and then of their congregations:

> Then what are these principles of heavenly communion? *Loving all whom Christ loves* (my italics) because they bear His impress; let this same rule then decide the question as to the subjects of our communion here on earth; all whom Christ loves, who bear His impress, or whom we ourselves acknowledge as Christians. Should we be asked how are these to be distinguished? We might hope the Holy Ghost will help us here; but at all events, not so much by agreement in those points which are the subjects of intellectual perception, as those which are embraced by a hearty and generous affection towards the Father for His love; towards the Son, for His unspeakable self-sacrificing humiliation; and to the Holy Spirit, for His aid and helps along our arduous, tottering course, till we are presented faultless before the Son of Man, at His appearing.
>
> Should it be asked what are to be done with errors? Are they not to bar communion? No; unless they bar Christ from the temple of the erring brother's heart. While we hope Christ lingers,

15

let us linger; and rather be behind than before to quit, in pitiful remembrance of our own iniquities and unnumbered errors. So long as we judge Christ to be dwelling with a man, that is our warrant for receiving him; and for the charity of that judgment that declares Him not there, we are responsible.

The first duty to ourselves is in selecting the congregation with whom we should statedly worship; it should be where the form is most scriptural in our persuasion, and the ministrations most spiritual; where there is the sweetest savour of Christ; where our own souls are most edified; where the Lord is most manifestly present with those who minister and those who hear. This is what we owe the Lord, the Church of God, and our own souls. Considering, however, agreement in what we think best as to form of worship altogether secondary to heart-agreement in the mystery of Christ and of godliness. These, then, appear the principles that ought to govern our selection, as individuals, of the place where we statedly worship, since personally we cannot be with all. Yet as to our liberty in Christ to worship with any congregation under heaven where He manifests Himself to bless and to save, can there be in any Christian mind a doubt? If my Lord should say to me, in any congregation of the almost unnumbered sections of the Church, 'What dost thou here?' I would reply, 'Seeing Thou wert here to save and sanctify, I felt it safe to be with Thee.' If He again said, as perhaps He may among most of us, 'Didst thou not see abominations here, an admixture of that which was unscriptural, and in some points error, at least in your judgment?' my answer would be, 'Yea, Lord, but I dared not call that place unholy where Thou wert present to bless, nor by refusing communion in worship reject those as unholy whom Thou hadst by Thy saving power evidently sanctified and set apart for Thine own.' Our reason for rejecting the congregations of apostate bodies is, that Christ doth not manifest Himself among them in their public character, though He may save some individuals as brands plucked from the burning. To these churches we cry, standing on the outside, 'Come out of her, my people; come out of her.'

To the question, 'Are we not countenancing error by this plan?' our answer is, that if we must appear to countenance

error, or discountenance brotherly love, and the visible union of
the Church of God, we prefer the former, hoping that our lives
and our tongues may be allowed by the Lord so intelli-
gibly to speak that at last our righteousness shall be allowed to
appear ... so long as Christ dwells in an individual, or walks in the
midst of a congregation, blessing the ministrations to the conver-
sion and edification of souls, we dare not denounce and formally
withdraw from either, for fear of the awful sin of schism, of sin
against Christ and His mystical body.[1]

This book is not about Evangelical compromise

Far from it. It often seems to me that the ecumenical movement begins at the lowest common denominator and builds
from that foundation a structure of brave words and empty
platitudes with the consequent inevitable compromise. I
have no truck with that. What is said here is addressed to
Evangelical Christians in the historical sense of the word.

Today the word 'evangelical' has become respectable,
even desirable, among an ever-widening circle. Therefore it
is essential that we understand its meaning. There have
always been areas of disagreement among Christians. There
are differences in the gospel ordinances, style of worship,
and church polity. The charismatic movement now touches
every aspect of evangelical life – and beyond it. For charismatic Christians to deny what they believe to be a new
work, a fresh revelation from the Lord by his Spirit, would
be to compromise. For others the practical ramification of
the renewal movement is a compromise as it embraces
those in non-Evangelical traditions. But from the opposite
end of the Evangelical spectrum yet more strident calls for
further separation have been sounded in the last few years.
Compromise is the word that we hear on every hand. Confusion has led to fear, and fear to mistrust, and mistrust to
statements and stances which have brought no glory to
Christ.

17

I am not offering firm solutions to these problems, but suggestions as to how they might be handled, how confidence can be built up and bridges constructed. However, this will not be by compromising the truth revealed in the word of God. We must be honest in our resolve, frank in what we say, yet also rebuilding trust. The truth must be held in love, but it must be held firmly.

This book is not about Evangelical uniformity

It is not a plea for some new association of like-minded people. I am fully identified with and committed to organisations such as the Evangelical Alliance. It is a plea that we hold fast to that which is good, and in those places where we believe God has placed us, but stop reproaching and recriminating one another. How easily we pigeon-hole those who have other emphases in their spirituality, and how quickly dismiss legitimate expressions of worship that are not our own. That I find some charismatic choruses trite and that charismatics find some of my hymns laboured and dull is not the point.

In Duke Street we try to accommodate many forms of worship. None is unanimously appreciated. There is criticism from young and old, traditionalists and 'modernists' (in worship, not doctrine!) – but that is nothing new. Have we forgotten that the verse-and-chorus style of hymns popularised by Moody and Sankey were brazen imitations of the ballads of the day? And I am just a little sceptical of the accusation of 'vain repetition' from those who like myself are prepared to sing a chorus six times during the course of one hymn. There is need for give and take on all sides.

Is the solution, then, in some agreed form of worship that caters for all tastes and viewpoints? No. Let traditional forms of worship continue. Dare I suggest, as one who is on many different platforms, that much 'charismatic' worship is as predictable as any other?

The heart of true worship is to speak of a holy God, recount his attributes, record his works of grace; to lay oneself open before his revealed word, and to walk in ways of his choosing. In true worship we are both brought by repentance and faith to the foot of the cross. On the last great day we shall both give an account at the throne of God and sit together in heavenly places. Whether the worship there will be to your taste or mine, I don't know, but having knelt where you have knelt at the cross, I must stand and sit where you will stand and sit so we can lift our united voices in love, praise and worship. And we must begin at once. Although certain forms of worship may not appeal to us, they may nevertheless be a worthy expression of praise for the blood-bought children of God, whether on synthesisers, with drums or the unaccompanied singing of metrical psalms. We can join together in praise with our brothers and sisters in Christ. Unless we kneel together in earnest pleading at the throne of grace for mercy in these desperate days, and sit together as a loving demonstration of the love of God to a loveless society, and stand together in proclamation of the gospel, the judgement of God will be unleashed upon us.

This book is not a theological text book

For that you will have to look elsewhere. But it will appeal to Scripture constantly. It will stand or fall at the bar of Holy Writ.

In the book *C.H. Spurgeon and the Modern Church* (London, Grace Publication Trust, 1985), R.J. Sheehan, drawing parallels with the situation today and Spurgeon's Downgrade Controversy, argues a case for separation. In his Preface, he blandly states that 'as this book is an historical survey, readers should not expect to find detailed exposition of Scripture to justify C.H. Spurgeon's stand. Detailed

exegetical argument will have to be present elsewhere.'
Sheehan is quite right – the book is largely free of biblical
references. If his was a work of historical research alone,
then he would be quite justified in his position. But it is not.
Whether the situation that Spurgeon faced and the situation
today are parallel or that conclusions can be drawn from one
to the other is questionable. Whether he is correct factually
is also questionable. But whatever, he is addressing himself to
the modern church in general and churches of the independent tradition in particular. His interest is not the Downgrade Controversy but the present situation and he addresses
himself to it. He has a perfect right to do so, but not apart
from the Bible.

Separation is undoubtedly taught in Scripture, and we will
be looking at what it means and how it is to be worked out.
However, the Bible teaches more on the unity of true believers than on their separation, more on their basic oneness
than on their differences. Let our only criterion be, not the
traditions of the elders, the historic emphasis of any constituency, the stance of certain forceful leaders, my place and
personal security in the group, but what the Bible says and
my response to it.

This book is not written by an authority on these matters

I was invited to write it by others, nevertheless, it is written
from a full heart. The contents are felt deeply. What are my
credentials? Providence alone. Having been brought up in
an Evangelical Baptist church with a nominal membership of
the Baptist Union, I trained at the independent Bible Training Institute in Glasgow and subsequently at Spurgeon's College. Some of my family have a strong influence in Evangelical Anglicanism. When my family are at home in Cornwall
we worship in a Methodist church. I have ministered in
churches of the Baptist Union and, until recently, in a Strict

Baptist Church in affiliation with the Association of Grace
Baptist Churches. I have the privilege of speaking on many
different platforms with links into several groupings.

From all this I have come to the conclusion that there is
much suspicion engendered by ignorance. Various misguided public utterances from one constituency percolate
through to another, fostering misunderstanding that grows
into mistrust. As some have spoken of their hopes and many
more of their fears, the need for a book on Evangelical unity
has become obvious. I speak of what I know and tell of what
I have seen.

2

Unity between Whom?

The word 'Evangelical' has a wide range of meanings. On the continent it is almost synonymous with 'Protestant'. Here it is applied to those who would not always be natural bed-fellows. Unless we understand who is being addressed, among whom this unity is to be demonstrated, then little will be achieved.

It would be wonderful if, in the goodness of God, unity might be realised among all who are 'in Christ' wherever they may be, whatever title they hold or denominational hat they wear. But that is beyond my wildest dreams, let alone faith, to believe. We are commissioned to go to all nations with the gospel so that all men might hear, turn and be saved, but in reality our expectation is less. So it is with unity. The Saviour prayed 'that all of them may be one'. Nevertheless, we set our sights a little lower than that. I speak of Evangelical unity – unity among those who firmly and honestly hold the histori-cally understood, biblical fundamentals of the faith.

Some will object that I am setting my terms of reference higher than the Scriptures demand. It has been said that the New Testament requirement to make one part of the body of Christ was the baptismal affirmation 'Jesus is Lord'. Why make the requirement for unity more restrictive than that? Professor Donald MacLeod would at first seem to support this argument. Writing in *Evangel* (Autumn 1985, pp. 2–10), a quarterly review of Biblical, practical and contemporary theology, he points out both the speed of entry into the church and the minimum confession required. Philip said to the Ethiopian eunuch, asking if anything prevented him from being baptised, 'If you believe with all your heart, you may.' The eunuch answered, 'I believe that Jesus Christ is the Son of God' (see Acts 8). On the Day of Pentecost, when the gathered people had been convicted by Peter's words, they cried out for spiritual help, 'accepted his message [and] were baptised' (Acts 2:41). Afterwards they continued to attend the Apostles' instruction, they shared in the fellowship and they participated in the breaking of bread and in prayer (Acts 2:42). 'The remedy lay not in undue scrutiny at the point of admission but in the application of discipline to unruly members,' says Professor MacLeod.

So why detail the requirement for entry, and thus restrict it? May I say that I am not so impertinent as to judge who is a true Christian and who is not – only God can do that. However, I address without apology those commonly described as Evangelical. They are my concern, and they alone are addressed in this book.

So who are Evangelicals? They are those who believe and practise the fundamental doctrines of the Bible. And what are those doctrines? Again I turn to Professor MacLeod: 'The fundamental doctrines are those without which we cannot live to the glory of God, come to maturity in faith, experience Biblical sanctification or live lives of obedience.' Drawing on such passages as Acts 17:1ff., 1 Corinthians 15:3, 14, and Galatians 1:8, MacLeod states that they are:

(1) Those doctrines on which the Scripture speaks with unmistakable clarity.
(2) Those doctrines which the New Testament specifically affirms to be fundamental.

(3) Those doctrines which are enshrined in the great creeds of the church or the doctrines believed by all Christians always and everywhere.

Rather than endeavouring some form of irreducible minimum, MacLeod lists eighteen such fundamental truths:

(1) The unity, spirituality, personal nature, holiness and graciousness of God.
(2) The doctrine of creation, especially the creation of man in the image of God.
(3) The fall and depravity of man.
(4) Man's accountability to God at a final judgement.
(5) The authority of the Scriptures.
(6) Vicarious atonement by the sacrifice of Christ.
(7) The resurrection of Christ.
(8) Justification by faith alone.
(9) The resurrection of the body.
(10) The consubstantial deity of Christ (Look it up!).
(11) The true and perfect humanity of Christ.
(12) The virgin birth of Christ.
(13) The ascension.
(14) The second coming.
(15) The church as a divine institution, marked by unity, holiness and universality.
(16) The consubstantial deity and authentic personal nature of the Holy Spirit.
(17) The fatherhood of God.
(18) The life everlasting.

'Come off it,' I hear you exclaim. 'Do you mean to say that a simple believer must understand all that, let alone believe it, before there can be unity in the Spirit?' Not exactly, but let me ask you this, has a church that believes in the above ever found that such beliefs have divided it, torn it to pieces, setting one group against another? Never. Why are creeds and statements of faith so distrusted and despised today? Some say it is arrogant to demand that someone believes certain requirements before they can be considered a Christian. Others say it is foolish to believe that an intellectual assent to a list of vaguely understood, archaic definitions can lead to a vibrant unity in Christ. How many say the Apostles' Creed 'with their fingers crossed behind their backs', to quote from a recent debate in the Synod of the Church of England? How useful are statements of faith when people cheat themselves, let alone God? I am aware of this. I am addressing here people who have truly experienced the saving work of Christ, who have been born again of the Spirit, and who trust in the word of God as his inspired revelation containing all that is necessary for us to know the saving purposes of God.

'But doctrine divides rather than unites,' comes the reply. 'The whole of church history proves it.' It does not. I quote MacLeod for the last time here:

> In fact, in many instances, it would be hypocrisy to claim that our divisions had anything to do with doctrinal consideration at all. Many of them have been the result of differences of opinion on matters of Church government, worship and discipline: of disputes on baptism, exclusive psalmody, and relations with the state. How many churches are split-offs from other churches and owe their existence to nothing more honourable than clashes of personality?

We will be looking at the differences mentioned by MacLeod in the following pages.

So then, those who are addressed here are those who are in basic agreement on the fundamentals of the faith as generally and unequivocally understood from the Holy Scriptures.

3

Christian Unity in the New Testament

In chapter 1 I emphasised the importance of listening to what Scripture says. If the weight of its teaching is separation – and Scripture certainly speaks about this – then we must be obedient to what it says. But if it condemns a sectarian spirit and places its over-riding emphasis on the manifested unity of the people of God, then should we do the same? Of course we should. The crux of the matter is the practical outworking of what we believe to be the main emphasis of Scripture. Whenever a situation crops up that brings serious concern to Christians – and there are many such concerns in the body of Christ – it is our duty to bring the Scriptures to that situation and that situation to the Scriptures. The matter is to be weighed in the scales of the Bible alone. We should not search for verses to support our particular position, to add credence to our course of action, but look for the over-riding force of biblical teaching. Many of us, having followed the above course of action, have discovered schism to be a fearful thing, and separation, other than on cardinal grievances which are clearly against the revealed will of God, something to be strictly avoided.

First, we will turn to the central New Testament passage on Christian unity as recorded in the high priestly prayer of Jesus in John 17:20–23:

> My prayer is not for them alone. I pray also for those who will believe in me through their message, that all of them may be one, Father, just as you are in me and I am in you. May they also be in us so that the world may believe that you have sent me. I have given them the glory that you gave me, that they may be one as we are one: I in them and you in me. May they be brought to complete unity to let the world know that you sent me and have loved them even as you have loved me.

This passage is quoted in almost every ecumenical exercise, but it cannot and dare not be discounted because of this. It was prayed by the Saviour and recorded by the Spirit for a purpose.

What is the context of this passage? The Saviour has spoken of his own relationship with the Father (Jn 17:1–5), he has prayed especially for his disciples – the eleven (Jn 17:6–19), and now he prays for all believers in all ages. 'I pray also for those who will believe in me through their message' – that is the elect in every age. And the force of that prayer is 'that all of them may be one'. The essence of the unity is so real, so heavenly in character and so far reaching in effect that it is, prays Jesus to his Father, 'just as you are in me and I am in you.' To deny the spiritual unity of every one who is in Christ is to deny the Godhead itself. But judging from some of today's statements and attitudes that appears to be happening.

What is the practical outworking, the importance of Jesus' prayer that we 'be brought to complete unity'? It is 'to let the world know that you sent me and have loved them even as you have loved me'. That the world may know. Unity is as vitally important as that. Yet for all the triumphalism in some quarters and the striving for a pure church in others, this nation knows less today of the love of the Father and the saving claims of Christ than at any time since the beginning of the Evangelical Awakening of the eighteenth century.

Why is this? The gospel is moving in great power around the world, but that is plainly not the case here in Britain. The reason is clear. There is little unity, let alone the complete unity of which Christ speaks. Large sections of 'the church' have prostituted the faith, diluted the gospel and gone chasing after other gods, while the blood-bought children of God are pursuing their own ends and, where they differ from their brethren, denouncing them and separating from them as a consequence. We have a grave responsibility. Recently E.J. Poole-Connor has been extensively quoted to endorse a 'separatist' position. But his book *Evangelical Unity* argues a different case. This great man of God, much used in the formation and subsequent direction of the Fellowship of Independent Evangelical Churches, makes some key points. He says, 'Aloofness, exclusiveness, schism – these things are as alien to our Lord's ideal of His Church as darkness is from light. It was, moreover, to be a unity which should compel the world to believe, in other words a unity so palpable as to be visible even to the purblind.'[2]

Three times the Saviour prayed, 'That all of them may be one,' 'That they may be one as we are one,' 'May they be brought to complete unity.' He did not pray for 'uniformity' – there is a diversity of role and ministry within the Godhead. Nor did he pray that the individual mind and conscience should cease to exist. The great Shepherd of the sheep left the body of the flock in search of the one lost sheep – the individual is of vital importance. Handley Moule remarks:

While the thought of the unit is banished from the plan of His Church, the thought of the unity is its characteristic glory. His gospel does indeed make the individual great, even to its utmost greatness. But the very essence of that greatness, according to Jesus Christ, demands that the man shall never *'terminate in himself'* but shall exist – in an existence supremely large and good – for others, in the Lord.... It is a common life of love, love

29

generated by the love of Him who is, eternally and within himself love. And love by its nature 'seeks its bliss in another's good', therefore love, by a most faithful law, results in unity itself.[3]

This is to be worked out in very practical ways among us. With those who have accepted the instructions given them by Christ – 'For I gave them the words you gave me and they accepted them' (Jn 17:18); with those who have the joy of Christ in them (Jn 17:13); with those who are hated by the world (Jn 17:14); with those who are being (the tense is present continuous) sanctified by the truth of God's word, and have been sent into the world (Jn 17:18) Jesus also prayed, 'Holy Father, protect them by the power of your name – the name you gave me – so that they may be one as we are one' (Jn 17:11). The whole of Christ's high priestly prayer is applicable to true believers. He does not pray for the disciples alone, so what he prays for them he prays for us.

John 17 has little to say of external unity and nothing to say of uniformity, but this does not imply that we should avoid considering the matter. Divisions have no value in themselves – far from it! I know a church of great importance to me – an altogether biblical church, in a small community, which split into two in that locality due to conflicting reasons. There were many real problems. The problems were apparently intractable, the outcome after a point inevitable. But was God glorified in it? What must have been the impression given to that community? Was the gospel furthered? I think not. Such disunity must be one of the main reasons why society is negative to the claims of Christ. Perhaps God refuses to use one section of his divided church as against another lest one should imply that it alone has his mind and will.

Turning to the epistles in this far from exhaustive overview, we discover several key passages.

Ephesians 4:3 – 'Make every effort to keep the unity of the Spirit through the bond of peace.' This clearly refers to a spiritual unity that is a reality for all true believers.

1 Corinthians 12:12–13 – 'The body is a unit, though it is made up of many parts; and though all its parts are many, they form one body. So it is with Christ. For we were all baptised by one Spirit into one body – whether Jews or Greeks, slave or free – and we were all given the one Spirit to drink.' It is a unity that requires our every effort to maintain.

Romans 12:5 – 'So in Christ we who are many form one body, and each member belongs to all the others.'

These verses speak not of a hope for the future, nor of a position to be achieved, but of a fact of present experience. Are you in Christ? If so, you are members of the same body (as an arm is a member of the body, not an organisation such as a golf club) as others who are in Christ, and we all have a mutual responsibility to each other. You may find my part in the body of Christ an embarrassment, not to your taste or liking at all, but here am I and there are you. There is a lot of talk about second degree separation today, as we shall see later, but if the Scriptures above reveal God's mind on unity, then certain things follow. E.J. Poole-Connor quotes D.M. Paton:

> No divergence of doctrine or ritual or practice can destroy a union which is based on life; nor is it possible to be unchurched by intellectual error when our organic union is fathoms deeper than intellectual. Unity in doctrine is impossible, unity in taste and sentiment is impossible; unity in attainment and experience is impossible; but unity in life is not only possible: it is a fact.[4]

So anything goes then. We are at liberty to believe and act as we like. Hardly. Ephesians 4:13 speaks of a unity that is yet to be – 'until we all reach unity in the faith and in the knowledge of the Son of God and become mature, attaining to the whole measure of the fulness of Christ.' This is not a unity that neglects God's word, that reduces the faith to the lowest possible common denominator – that is a sham, a caricature of what Paul had in mind. The oneness of which he speaks is described in Ephesians 4:4–5 – 'There is one body and one Spirit – just as you were called to one hope when you were called – one Lord, one faith, one baptism.' Let's look more closely at the oneness which Paul describes.

One body

Paul elaborates on this later in the chapter.

> Then we will not longer be infants, tossed back and forth by the waves, and blown here and there by every wind of teaching and by the cunning and craftiness of men in their deceitful scheming. Instead, speaking the truth in love, we will in all things grow up into him who is the Head, that is, Christ. From him the whole body, joined and held together by every supporting ligament, grows and builds itself up in love, as each part does its work (Eph 4:14–16).

The body of Christ is the church, not the building on the corner with a peeling notice board and the announcement of Christmas services in March. It is a unified whole – comparable to a building, a bride, a physical body – made up of all those in Christ. You cannot deny others in the body, even though you consider some of them to be unpresentable (1 Cor 12). There should be no division in the body. There are certainly differences in the body. Gifts vary, but God distributes all of them among different believers: 'There are different kinds of working, but the same God works all of them in all men' (1 Cor 12:6).

One Spirit

Every true believer has been born again of the Spirit. Jesus said, 'The wind blows wherever it pleases. You hear its sound, but you cannot tell where it comes from or where it is going. So it is with everyone born of the Spirit' (Jn 3:8). Paul wrote: 'You, however, are controlled not by the sinful nature but by the Spirit, if the Spirit of God lives in you. And if anyone does not have the Spirit of Christ, he does not belong to Christ' (Rom 8:9).

These scriptures imply that if we do not count as a Christian someone in whom a work of grace has clearly begun by the Spirit, we are arguing with the sovereignty of God. In fact, we are denying Christ in that one, and that is very serious. The words of the Lord Jesus are solemn: 'Whoever disowns me before men, I will disown him before my Father in heaven' (Mt 10:33).

One hope

Hope in the New Testament is that certain assurance of the reality of a thing not yet realised. New Testament hope is not fingers crossed and touch wood, but rather the final work of redemption which has not yet been fully accomplished but for which we long. The Saviour prays for every believer: 'Father, I want those you have given me to be with me where I am, and to see my glory, the glory you have given me because you loved me before the creation of the world' (Jn 17:24). That hope when realised will certainly be shared. Handley Moule says that a 'prepared place demands a prepared people'. Part of that preparation is to accept those whom Christ has accepted, to live now with those he wants us to share eternity with.

One Lord

The Lordship of Christ is crucial to unity. If he is Lord then we should submit to his teaching and not discount what he deems to be important or ignore what he has revealed of the

Father. In the same prayer that Jesus says, 'I have given them your word' (Jn 17:14), he also prays that we might be one. In Romans 10 Paul speaks to those who by confession and belief declare Jesus to be Lord and are saved. '"Anyone who trusts in him will never be put to shame." For ... the same Lord is Lord of all and richly blesses all who call on him, for, "Everyone who calls on the name of the Lord will be saved"' (Rom 10:11–12). Among 'all who call on him' you will find some very strange bedfellows, but who are we to argue against the wisdom and love of God in whom he calls?

One faith

In the hymn 'The church's one foundation', we sing heartily that her 'charter of salvation' includes 'one faith', but is your 'one faith' the same as mine? Is it an irreducible minimum by which a man must be saved? Dr Wayne Detzler in his book *Living Words in Ephesians* (Welwyn, Evangelical Press, 1981) describes it as 'an elementary body of Biblical doctrine – the deity of Christ, His substitutionary atonement and His resurrection from the dead'. Personally, I could not envisage a reduction greater than that. Jude wrote, 'I ... urge you to contend for the faith that was once for all entrusted to the saints' (Jude 3).

There are elements over which Bible-believing Christians disagree, but none of us can be so absolutely sure that we possess the sole truth so as to condemn the actions of some and the witness of others.

> Will any man outside Rome have the hardihood to claim that the religious assembly to which he belongs is alone infallible? The very fact that there are divergences should inculcate humility. The utmost that anyone can say is that his creed is a statement of Scriptural truth *as he sees it* and, therefore, binding on his own conscience. To attempt to make it binding on that of his

34

brethren, and to exclude them from communion because their interpretation of the 'one faith' is different from his, is to claim for an exegesis of Scripture the infallibility of Scripture itself.[5]

It is strange that Poole-Connor should be widely quoted in a recent book supporting second degree separation. He quotes Richard Baxter in *The Reformed Pastor* who knew very well the cost of contending for the gospel: 'We must learn to distinguish between certainties and uncertainties, necessaries and unnecessaries, Catholic verities and private opinions, and to lay the stress of the Church's peace upon the former, not upon the latter.' If anything has convinced me of the grievous spirit of the present time it has been reading *Evangelical Unity*. This book, actually published by the Fellowship of Independent Evangelical Churches, could have come from another age in comparison with the climate today into which some who would count themselves to be in his succession have entered. In actual fact the book was first published as recently as 1941. Perhaps we have entered a new ice age since then. I almost catch the cry of Paul to the Galatians: 'I am astonished that you are so quickly deserting the one who called you by the grace of Christ and are turning to a different gospel' (Gal 1:6).

One baptism

Paul isn't joking here, so neither should we. Save to say there *is* only one baptism (Mt 28:19), let our conviction be conviction and our practice practice, according to our understanding of Scripture. In this area there must be mutual love and tolerance – and thank God that in large measure there is. Both the Evangelical Alliance and the British Evangelical Council are made up of paedobaptists and those practising believers' baptism. No one who has read *The Biblical Doctrine of Infant Baptism* (Cambridge, James Clarke, 1953) by

Pierre Ch. Marcel will dismiss infant baptism with a quip. We only have to read men of God such as Jonathan Edwards, who loathed anabaptists, to understand that great strides have been made in growing trust and understanding since the eighteenth century. We will be looking more closely at evangelical unity on this point of baptism, for it is not a secondary issue. Around the baptism question revolves not a difference of practice but a completely different theological viewpoint. If Evangelicals have learnt to live together here, at perhaps our most vulnerable point, can we not make a better effort for progress elsewhere?

One God and Father of all

Here it is again. All Christians belong to one family. If God is your Father, then I am your brother. Is, then, the only consideration for true fellowship to ascertain that someone is in Christ, if that were possible? Obviously not. Is a mini-confession sufficient for ministry and evangelism? Far from it. However, if another is in Christ we have certain responsibilities towards him that cannot be brushed aside. Christ received us as sinners saved by grace and that is how we are to receive each other. 'Accept one another,' Paul wrote, 'just as Christ accepted you, in order to bring praise to God' (Rom 15:7). We dare not ask more than Christ asked. Repentance and faith in the finished work of Christ, itself the gift of God, made me one with Christ.

Grace and love should mark our attitude to others who, like us, are 'debtors to mercy alone'. The following scriptures give the criteria for general fellowship between Christians:

'Be devoted to one another, in brotherly love. Honour one another above yourselves' (Rom 12:10). 'My command is this: Love each other as I have loved you' (Jn 15:12). 'Now a slave has no permanent place in the family, but a son belongs to it for ever' (Jn 8:35). 'To all who received him who believed in his name, he gave the right to become children of God – children

36

born not of natural descent, nor of human decision or a husband's will, but born of God' (Jn 1:12–13).

Along these criteria, we should be as embracing as we can. However, for that intimacy of fellowship that is the feature of the local church, the boundaries have to be drawn more tightly. This is not to deny that others outside our fellowship are not in Christ. It is simply that a local church must enjoy fellowship around a certain understanding of Christian doctrine and on the basis of our mutual acceptance of the word of God, its teaching, practice and discipline. This was the very lovely basis of faith of my church in Bournemouth:

> We, a body of sinners saved through the grace of God, do hereby unite in Church Fellowship, so that as a holy brotherhood, we may advocate the truth of God, proclaim the riches of His sovereign mercy to the lost and perishing, and by sympathy and counsel help one another in the Christlike and heavenward life. We believe it our privilege and duty, by the Spirit's aid, to bear one another's burdens, and in the exercise of a tender-hearted, tolerant, forgiving kindliness, to avoid everything of harsh and ungenerous criticism, recognising in each other fellow-members of that mystical body of which our risen Saviour is the Head. We seek to maintain in primitive simplicity, purity of worship and communion. We regard as essential features in the teaching of our Lord Jesus Christ that redeemed souls should walk in newness of life and holy separation from the world; and consider those only admissible to the Lord's Table who profess their sins forgiven through the blood of Jesus, and whose lives are in harmony with that great truth.
>
> While desiring to extend to all believers the fullest and freest liberty of conscience, we require from all Church members an adhesion to the following doctrines of our faith as understood in a simple and straightforward and evangelical sense:
> (1) The plenary inspiration, sole authority and all-sufficiency of the Holy Scriptures as originally given.
> (2) The trinity in unity of the Godhead.
> (3) The essential deity and perfect humanity of our Lord Jesus Christ.

(4) The personality of the Holy Spirit.

(5) The depraved and fallen state of man through Adam's transgression.

(6) Atonement through the substitutionary death-sacrifice and blood-shedding of the Lord Jesus Christ.

(7) The justification of the sinner through faith in the risen Christ.

(8) The personality of the Devil.

(9) The second advent of our Lord Jesus Christ.

(10) The resurrection of the body.

(11) The natural immortality of the soul.

(12) The everlasting security of the believer, and the everlasting punishment of those who die impenitent.

(13) The perpetuity of the Ordinance of Baptism of believers by immersion in water on confession of each individual of faith in the Lord Jesus Christ.

(14) The Ordinance of the Lord's Supper, thereby showing forth in the simple emblems of the broken bread and poured out wine, 'the Lord's death, till He come.'

When local churches are formed where people covenant together in fellowship, a basis more binding is clearly necessary than for wider relationships. But even this is not to deny anything of another's standing in Christ, but to say that this for us is the basis of our covenanting together in fellowship. A basis of faith is not only necessary for fellowship in the local church, but also for evangelism. How can you evangelise with those who do not share the same experience of the evangel?

But on all this where do we draw the line? The problem of Evangelical unity is that rather than finding those areas of common agreement, the boundaries are constantly being contracted, the perimeter walls heightened, and the restrictions and bars to fellowship intensified. 1 Peter 1:22 is of great importance here: 'Now that you have purified yourselves by obeying the truth' – indeed we have, say some, with a degree of satisfaction – 'so that you have sincere love for your brothers, love one another deeply, from the heart.' It is sad and disturbing that so often those who speak most of obeying the truth (as they understand it) seem to be the ones who lack in startling measure its corollary, loving one another deeply from the heart. Something has gone wrong somewhere. 'If I speak in the tongues of men and of angels, but have not love...' (1 Cor 13:1). To read the Evangelical press and to attend some of the conferences is to discover the very antithesis of 1 Corinthians 13:4–7:

> Love is patient, love is kind. It does not envy, it does not boast, it is not proud. It is not rude, it is not self-seeking, it is not easily angered, it keeps no record of wrongs. Love does not delight in evil but rejoices with the truth. It always protects, always trusts, always hopes, always perseveres.

In defence of their attitude some point to a contrived emotionalism that is a substitute for true love. The love of Jesus should be tangible among us, we should be able to describe it at work among us. Love is always corporate – it seeks its object. That is the proof of love.

It is a salutary discovery that the New Testament speaks much more of the sin of schism than it ever does of the errors of compromise. As we shall see later, second degree separation is based on the flimsiest of scriptural exegesis, while the whole weight of scriptural evidence is on the essential responsibility we have to 'make every effort to keep the unity of the Spirit through the bond of peace' (Eph 4:3).

There are many commands to withhold from those whose conduct is contrary to the Christian walk. Evangelical unity is not a denial of church discipline. In fact it can only really be accomplished among those where it is exercised. Paul wrote:

> You must not associate with anyone who calls himself a brother but is sexually immoral or greedy, an idolater or a slanderer, a drunkard or a swindler. With such a man do not even eat (1 Cor 5:11).

In the name of the Lord Jesus Christ, we command you, brothers, to keep away from every brother who is idle and does not live according to the teaching you received from us.... We hear that some among you are idle. They are not busy; they are busybodies.... If anyone does not obey our instruction in this letter, take special note of him. Do not associate with him, in order that he may feel ashamed. Yet do not regard him as an enemy, but warn him as a brother (2 Thess 3:6, 11, 14, 15).

Even then, when sin is clearly evident, careful instruction is given: 'Brothers, if someone is caught in a sin, you who are spiritual should restore him gently. But watch yourself, or you also may be tempted (Gal 6:1). The lazy brother of 2 Thessalonians 3:6 is not to be regarded as an enemy but warned as a brother.

But nothing is said regarding instructions for dividing from a brother (by brother, I mean a child of God) who holds differing views or emphases or association from yourself. Rather, the heaviest censure falls on the troubler of the flock, the disturber of the peace, the one who would distort or divide the body of Christ.

Galatians 5:20–21 speaks of the 'acts of the sinful nature'. These include 'hatred, discord, jealousy, fits of rage', and then, 'selfish ambition, dissensions, factions' (that is, parties within the church). Paul states that 'those who live like this will not inherit the kingdom of God'. That is serious. To be a troubler of the fellowship, a party within the church, is to bring your very standing in Christ into question.

In the same letter Paul wrote: 'When Peter came to Antioch, I opposed him to his face, because he was clearly in the wrong' (Gal 2:11). And he an apostle at that! It was because 'he began to draw back and separate himself from the Gentiles because he was afraid...' (Gal 2:12). Because of his fear of the powerful, influential Judaisers in Jerusalem he was disobedient. Fear is still a root cause of the problem of separation today. Because certain gifted and influential people who seek to separate the body of Christ have gained a hearing and a following, others have been dragged into their sin through fear. Integrity is attacked, a believer's spiritual standing questioned, his motives impugned, his fellowship resisted. From fear, those who are deeply uneasy and desperately troubled are hesitant of saying that enough is enough. As Peter discovered, first by vision and then by public rebuke, it is a terrible matter to 'call anything impure that God has made clean' (Acts 10:15).

So what is to be done about this sin? Titus 3:9–10 tells us very clearly: 'But avoid foolish controversies and genealogies and arguments and quarrels about the law, because these are unprofitable and useless. Warn a divisive person once, and then warn him a second time. After that, have nothing to do with him.' And again, in Romans 16:17: 'I urge you, brothers, to watch out for those who cause divisions and put obstacles in your way that are contrary to the teaching you have learned. Keep away from them.'

A divisive person is to be warned once and then warned a second time. Only after that are we to keep away from such people. But is not that in itself a denial of Evangelical unity? True unity will be among those who are obedient to the word of God, and the sin of division must be faced and dealt with for what it is.

To be a troubler of the fellowship is sin. The Bible is quite clear, and for that we must give an account. It is plainly a sin to dismiss as 'dead' a local fellowship struggling to maintain a witness, firm on the truth, and obedient to the light it has received, because it does not manifest the gifts as you understand them, or have the surface appeal that another's demonstrative worship engenders. To infiltrate a gospel church with the intention of changing it to your taste or emphasis is a sin. To manipulate its constitution and rules for your selfish purpose is an offence before God. I have heard of a church where a large section of the membership

41

has left but retained its 'membership' so as to influence the next choice of a minister. Such behaviour is totally unworthy, in fact reprehensible before God.

Again, to refuse fellowship with a people or their pastor because of some historical association or secondary divergence from your understanding, though theirs be manifestly a gospel church and ministry, is to run in total contradiction to the word of God and will bring judgement upon us:

> You, then, why do you judge your brother? Or why do you look down on your brother? For we will all stand before God's judgment seat. It is written: '"As surely as I live," says the Lord, "Every knee will bow before me; every tongue will confess to God."' So then, each of us will give an account of himself to God. Therefore let us stop passing judgment on one another. Instead, make up your mind not to put any stumbling-block or obstacle in your brother's way (Rom 14:10–13).

4

Biblical Separation

The Bible most certainly speaks of separation. Evangelical unity dare not be at the expense of the truth or by ignoring what is clearly taught in Scripture. It is among those who are 'in Christ' and under the word of God that unity is to be demonstrated, for although they may differ in their understanding, it will still be on the basis of what the Bible says.

Klaas Runia, writing in *Baker's Dictionary of Christian Ethics* (Grand Rapids, MI, Baker, 1973) draws a distinction between schism, separation and separatism. Schism, he argues, is 'a division without sufficient ground'. Separation he defines as the 'action of believers who separate themselves from their church because the latter has become unfaithful to the Word of God'. Separatism he sees as 'the attitude of those who, motivated by some form of ecclesiological perfectionism, leave their church'.

We will deal with the matter of schism and separation later under sectarianism. The purpose of this chapter is to differentiate between the separation that the Bible teaches and the separation of men, and how the former is to be encouraged and the latter avoided.

Separation from whom or what is, of course, the immediate question. Countless books have been written on the church, but before we go a step further a minimal definition must be given so as to avoid hopeless confusion later. The problem has arisen in that the English word 'Church' is derived from the Greek word *kyriakos* meaning 'The Lord's house' or a Christian place of worship, whereas the Greek word used in the New Testament, *ekklesia*, never means a building but rather a local congregation of the Lord's people. The *New Bible Dictionary* (Leicester, Inter-Varsity Press, 1982) helpfully points out that Tyndale always translated *ekklesia* as 'congregation'. It was not until the coming of the Authorised Version that 'congregation' was replaced by 'church'. Confusion has reigned ever since.

The debate continues as to whether the New Testament word *ekklesia* was derived from the Jewish or Gentile use of the word. Whatever, it means 'meeting' but not society, organisation, denomination, association or any such thing. From the *kyriakos* there can be a separation, but for the child of God there can be no separation from *ekklesia*. The Augsburg Confession describes the church as 'the assembly of all believers among whom the gospel is preached in its purity and the sacraments are administered according to the gospel'. The Westminster Confession puts it:

> The catholic or universal Church, which is invisible, consists of the whole number of the elect, that have been, are, or shall be gathered into one under Christ the Head thereof; and is the spouse, the body, the fulness of Him that filleth all in all.
>
> This catholic Church hath been sometimes more, sometimes less visible. And particular Churches, which are members thereof, are more or less pure, according as the doctrine of the Gospel is taught and embraced, ordinances administered, and public worship performed more or less purely in them.
>
> The purest Churches under heaven are subject both to mixture and error.

However, to say that there can be no separation from the *ekklesia* is not the end of the matter. For the Bible does speak of separation – while often essential it is always painful.

First, the Bible tells us that sin causes a separation between God and man: 'But your iniquities have separated you from your God; your sins have hidden his face from you, so that he will not hear' (Is 59:2). Sin is a terrible thing. It provokes the righteous judgement of God. It creates a chasm between God and man that only grace can bridge. That bridge is the cross – the sacrificial, substitutionary death of our Lord Jesus Christ. For those who are in Christ, those who know what it 'cost to make a sinner whole', they cannot and will not be blasé about sin. For those who have been redeemed 'not with perishable things such as silver or gold ... but with the precious blood of Christ' (1 Pet 1:18–19), perhaps the most painful of sins is a denial of the very work of Christ. From that we can but separate. Although the method and manner of Christ's work on the cross will be debated, the absolute necessity of it must surely be understood. Our unity in Christ, then, must also be a unity in this truth.

The first epistle of John addresses itself to this particular situation. The church to which John wrote had obviously suffered a grievous split, leaving people dreadfully confused. One section of the church had separated and formed a new group down the road. Which group was right? How was the truth to be ascertained? How could they possibly know the truth when both claimed to have the truth? Certainly, the schismatic group were very plausible. Apparently they claimed above all else such a degree of spiritual enlightenment as to make themselves 'without sin' (1 Jn 1:8). Such claims of special spiritual experiences and heightened awareness unknown and unavailable to ordinary folk always receive attention. But to his troubled readers John says, 'You can know!' There are tests we can apply which, under the Spirit of God, lead to Christ and then to assurance. Assurance is not arrogance or conceit, as some suppose, but the will of God for every true believer. And assurance is

45

always centred on the Saviour: 'I know whom I have believed, and am convinced that he is able...' (2 Tim 1:12).

John's first test is obedience

> Everyone who has this hope in him purifies himself, just as he is pure. Everyone who sins breaks the law; in fact, sin is lawlessness. But you know that he appeared so that he might take away our sins. And in him is no sin. No-one who lives in him keeps on sinning. No-one who continues to sin has either seen him or known him (1 Jn 3:3–6).
>
> Everyone who believes that Jesus is the Christ is born of God, and everyone who loves the father loves his child as well. This is how we know that we love the children of God: by loving God and carrying out his commands. This is love for God: to obey his commands. And his commands are not burdensome, for everyone born of God overcomes the world. This is the victory that has overcome the world, even our faith (1 Jn 5:1–4).

True believers seek to obey the commands of Christ. John wrote, 'But if anyone obeys his word, God's love is truly made complete in him' (1 Jn 2:5). Christ's commands are his clear, unequivocal purposes for men. These are contained in his words and the words of the Apostles which have been written down and preserved for us in God's word, the Bible. To deny the word, dilute it, change it or misapply it is a grievous sin, for it is changing the gospel. The Bible says, 'But even if we or an angel from heaven should preach a gospel other than the one we preached to you, let him be eternally condemned!' (Gal 1:8).

The gospel is not to be tampered with by men. What some say may sound wise, erudite and convincing. It surely did to those who had left the church to which John wrote. But plausibility is not the criterion. Paul addresses the same issue in writing to the Romans:

I urge you, brothers, to watch out for those who cause divisions and put obstacles in your way that are contrary to the teaching you have learned. Keep away from them. For such people are not serving our Lord Christ, but their own appetites. By smooth talk and flattery they deceive the minds of naïve people. Everyone has heard about your obedience, so I am full of joy over you; but I want you to be wise about what is good, and innocent about what is evil (Rom 16:17–19).

What thrills Paul about the believers in Rome is their obedience. They are keeping away from those who are 'contrary to the teaching you have learned'. Is some teaching new to you? Then be wary of it. Do not reject it at once, but weigh it against what you have already learned. Bring it to the test of Scripture.

John follows up this theme in his second epistle, where he is painfully frank:

Many deceivers, who do not acknowledge Jesus Christ as coming in the flesh, have gone out into the world. Any such person is the deceiver and the antichrist. Watch out that you do not lose what you have worked for, but that you may be rewarded fully. Anyone who runs ahead and does not continue in the teaching of Christ does not have God; whoever continues in the teaching has both the Father and the Son. If anyone comes to you and does not bring this teaching, do not take him into your house or welcome him. Anyone who welcomes him shares in his wicked work (2 Jn 7–11).

Not much love in that, I hear you say. But let me remind you that the one who writes probably knew more of love than any man there has ever been except Jesus. He is the 'Apostle of love'. That he is so blunt about false teaching shows how desperately serious the issue is. To stay away from it is a matter of obedience.

Incidentally, verse 10 does not mean a withdrawal of common courtesy or social humanity. Not to welcome someone in this context means not to identify with him and fraternise with him, thus giving the impression of agreeing with his pernicious teaching. This is why some of us would be hesitant about appearing on a platform with someone who is known to deny a fundamental doctrine. We are not against free speech, nor do we claim to have all truth. Nevertheless, we dare not imply endorsement of what might be said in contradiction to the truth we have received. Otherwise the impression will be given that what we hold dear is not really important, when for us all of eternity rests on it. E.J. Poole-Connor saw this quite clearly:

> The answer is that the writer distinguishes between church-fellowship and fellowship in public testimony; and while he believes that a creed is out of place as a condition of the former, he regards it as being very valuable in the case of the latter. A personal experience may illustrate the point. The writer was once discussing with his predecessor in the pastorate of the Talbot Tabernacle, the late Frank H. White, the theological position of a neighbouring minister, Dr John Clifford. 'I am aware,' said Mr White in effect, 'that Dr Clifford is, from our standpoint, unsound in his attitude to Holy Scripture, but we must never forget that he is a truly converted man, a fellow-member of the family of faith.' On the ground of this spiritual relationship, both pastors would have unhesitatingly sat down at the Lord's Table with him. Nevertheless, a year or two later the writer felt compelled to decline an invitation to take part in an evangelistic mission with the doctor (whose Modernist views of Scripture were then common knowledge) on the ground that to do so might lead to a verbal clash on the platform, or cause confusion in the public mind; either contingency being equally undesirable. For co-operation of this character some agreement on fundamentals is manifestly necessary: in other words, some common creed.[6]

Following on from this, it would seem to me an impossibility for a man to be identified with or a member of a denomination whose doctrinal position is in clear contradiction to the gospel. Sadly, even that is not as clearly understood by some as it should be. Much more complicated is when the official doctrinal position of a denomination is, in its essential points, according to the truth, but many within it – perhaps even the majority – do not subscribe to it, ignore it or contradict it. What then? We will look at this mattter again later.

John's second test is love

> Dear friends, I am not writing you a new command but an old one, which you have had since the beginning. This old command is the message you have heard. Yet I am writing you a new command; its truth is seen in him and you, because the darkness is passing and the true light is already shining.
>
> Anyone who claims to be in the light but hates his brother is still in the darkness. Whoever loves his brother lives in the light, and there is nothing in him to make him stumble. But whoever hates his brother is in the darkness and walks around in the darkness; he does not know where he is going, because the darkness has blinded him (1 Jn 2:7–11).

(See also 1 John 3:11–24 and 1 John 4:7–21.) The vital importance of this test is obvious from its exhaustive treatment. Note that obedience is not a contradiction of love, neither need love be at the cost of obedience. One of the most offensive characteristics of the present polarisation within evangelicalism is that each accuses the other of lovelessness. Why do we injure each other so? What does John say about love here? His words are clear, practical and desperately need to be applied to our situation today.

First, love is a command (1 Jn 2:7). If you are disobedient about love then you fail the previous test on obedience; that

49

is quite clear. For the obedient one, 'God's love is truly made complete in him. This is how we know we are in him' (1 Jn 2:5).

Secondly, this love is a matter of truth (1 Jn 2:8). True love is not wishy-washy sentimentality. It has to do with the darkness passing and the true light shining (1 Jn 2:8).

Thirdly, to hate one's brother, that fellow member of Christ's family (1 Jn 2:9), is still to be in darkness. A true believer will do nothing to make his brother stumble (1 Jn 2:10). Certainly he will not lead him into or encourage him in error. Neither by his attitude nor denial of the love of Christ will he cause his brother to fall. There is no doubt that many have been driven into the far country by lack of love at home. Finding a warmer, kinder place abroad they take up residence there, even though it is not the Father's house. The older brother of Luke 15 still lives.

Fourthly, we must not be like Cain and murder our brother, but love one another (1 Jn 3:12). The vindictive spirit and censorious attitude of the writing of some people has almost made me wonder if the second half of 1 John 3:14 is true of them: 'Anyone who does not love remains in death.' What other explanation can there be? It is not an either/or matter, truth or love. It is absolutely essential for there to be both. The three tests of 1 John are like a three-legged stool. Remove one and the whole thing topples over. It is a salient point that the question of love has by far the most exhaustive treatment in John's epistle. Among biblical Christians love is in desperately short supply.

Fifthly, true love means sacrifice (1 Jn 3:17–20). The love of the Saviour was terribly practical. It involved real sacrifice, real suffering, real death. And our love is to be something like that. Who are we to deserve such love? 'While we were still sinners, Christ died for us' (Rom 5:8). He loved the unlovely. It is easy to love our own group, to be aware of the needs of our own constituency, but if that had been the way of Christ, none of us would have been saved.

Lack of love is the abuse we throw at all who disagree with us. It is an easy jibe. For seven years I had the privilege of ministering among the Strict Baptists of Suffolk. Cold, doctrinaire, loveless, have been some of the words used in my hearing to describe them by those largely ignorant of them, knowing them only at a distance. I would have said much the same before God took me among them. It is a lie, of course, for they are the warmest and kindest people of experiential faith that I have been privileged to meet. A little insular, perhaps, but certainly most loving and supportive. I counted myself one of them and will always be glad of the opportunity to minister among them in the future.

Before I deny love in another, let me look for the evidence of Christ's love in me. Is it practical with regard to my brother's needs? Is it positive towards one who has had less opportunity than I? Is it understanding towards one who finds himself in an area and constituency different from mine and has to face pressures and problems which I don't? Is it constructive towards one who is hungering for more of the truth and is on pilgrimage in the faith? Does it seek to understand one who, believing himself to be obedient and faithful, has yet come to different conclusions on secondary issues? Does it seek to find the truth before it criticises? Does it seek to discover if the one with whom I disagree has more of Christ than I? If it does not do these things, it knows nothing of Calvary love. John makes it quite clear that if you belong to the truth you will be a very loving person (1 Jn 3:19).

Sixthly, the marriage of truth and love is established completely. The command of 1 John 3:23 to believe in the name of God's Son Jesus Christ is clearly shorthand for believing in his person, work and teaching and thus doing what he commands, which in this instance is to love one another.

All this is amplified and reapplied with great clarity in 1 John 4:7–21. We all declare that we love our fellow believers while the situation among biblical Christians tells us quite plainly that we do not. We have already diagnosed the problem – fear. Fear of another emphasis, fear of leaders, fear of the group, fear of what others will say. I repeat that writing this book has made me frightened of what some will say, frightened of being ostracised and censured by my brothers and sisters in Christ. But 'perfect love drives out fear' (1 Jn 4:18). Are you still confident that you love the children of God? You will know by applying the test of 'loving God and carrying out his commands' (1 Jn 5:2).

John's third test is doctrine

Dear children, this is the last hour; and as you have heard that the antichrist is coming, even now many antichrists have come (1 Jn 2:18). (See also 1 John 2:19–29; 4:1–6; 5:1–12.) Who the antichrist is and whether he will be an individual or the personification of evil is of no interest to us here. The much more pressing question is 'even now many antichrists have come'. Who are they, how can they be recognised, and how should they be avoided?

The test of antichrists is their relationship to the Lord Jesus Christ. Jesus himself said, 'He who is not with me is against me, and he who does not gather with me scatters' (Mt 12:30). You cannot be neutral about the Lord Jesus – you are either for him or against him. If a fellowship, however inadequate or divergent on secondary matters, seeks to enthrone him, then they are not to be avoided. But if a church – a modern-day Laodicea – is rich, successful, wonderfully supported, majestic in worship, superb in musical excellence, but leaves the Lord Jesus Christ on the outside – then it must be avoided like the plague. The test is the Lord Jesus Christ himself.

Antichrist teaching, then, must include:

(1) False Christs.
'Many will come in my name, claiming, "I am he,"
and will deceive many' (Mk 13:6).

(2) Distorters of the truth.
'I know that after I leave, savage wolves will come in
among you and will not spare the flock. Even from
your own number men will arise and distort the truth
in order to draw away disciples after them' (Acts
20:29–30).

(3) Deceivers.

> Concerning the coming of our Lord Jesus Christ and our
> being gathered to him, we ask you, brothers, not to
> become easily unsettled or alarmed by some prophecy,
> report or letter supposed to have come from us, saying
> that the day of the Lord has already come. Don't let
> anyone deceive you in any way, for that day will not
> come until the rebellion occurs and the man of lawless-
> ness is revealed, the man doomed to destruction. He
> opposes and exalts himself over everything that is called
> God or is worshipped, and even sets himself up in God's
> temple, proclaiming himself to be God (2 Thess 2:1–4).

They are forerunners of the antichrist par excellence,
the man of lawlessness, the man of sin.

(4) Those who abandon the faith to follow the 'deceiving
spirits and things taught by demons'.

'The Spirit clearly says that in later times some will abandon
the faith and follow deceiving spirits and things taught by
demons. Such teachings come through hypocritical liars, whose
consciences have been seared as with a hot iron' (1 Tim 4:1–2).

It is the responsibility of a good minister to point these
things out. A pastor who does not instruct his people about
the devil's tactics in seeking to dethrone Christ is failing those
for whom he has a responsibility. Paul told the Thessalonians:

'Don't you remember that when I was with you I used to tell you these things?' (2 Thess 2:5).

It is sobering that even in John's day, many antichrists had already come. We can hardly anticipate it being otherwise today. Who they are and how they are to be recognised, John makes quite clear: 'Who is the liar? It is the man who denies that Jesus is the Christ. Such a man is the antichrist – he denies the Father and the Son' (1 Jn 2:22).

So then, if someone declares himself to be the Christ, as did Sun Myung Moon, he is antichrist. Or if someone, though speaking the name of Christ, denies his person or work, he is antichrist. John tells us:

> This is how you can recognise the Spirit of God: Every spirit that acknowledges that Jesus Christ has come in the flesh is from God, but every spirit that does not acknowledge Jesus is not from God. This is the spirit of the antichrist, which you have heard is coming and even now is already in the world (1 Jn 4:2–3).

Or if another, even though he describes himself as a prophet, bishop or minister, opposes Christ and the things of Christ, he is also antichrist.

Here is the infallible test: 'What do you think of Christ?' The sentiments might be beautiful, the aspirations lofty, the prot-estations of orthodoxy strident, but if someone falls down as to what the Saviour says of himself and what the Bible clearly teaches concerning his pre-existent deity, virgin birth, sinless life, sacrificial atoning death, bodily resurrection, physical ascension, visible personal return and eternal reign, then he is against Christ. The denial of Christ has led to separation from the beginning: 'They went out from us, but they did not really belong to us. For if they had belonged to us, they would have remained with us; but their going showed that none of them belonged to us' (1 Jn 2:19).

Note that it is the false teachers who have excommunicated themselves. It is they who have left and us who remain. John

Stott says: 'The heretics went out of their own volition, but behind the secession was the divine purpose that the spurious should be made manifest, lest the elect should be led astray.'[7] Their departure was their unmasking. What is counterfeit cannot remain for ever hidden. Jesus said, 'For false Christs and false prophets will appear and perform great signs and miracles to deceive even the elect – if that were possible' (Mt 24:24). But the deceit will not be for long: 'His work will be shown for what it is, because the Day will bring it to light. It will be revealed with fire, and the fire will test the quality of each man's work' (1 Cor 3:13). I have come to the conclusion that if the denial of the person and work of Christ is not enough to cause a separation, then there is hardly likely to be any other issue. If an attack on the One who is everything and all in all is insufficient, then what will be?

From 1 John it is quite plain that where there are those who make no effort to follow the commands of Christ, where little or no evidence of Calvary love is to be seen, and where antichrists are discerned as being at work, then we must separate from them. But to what degree are we confident that in every respect we are what Christ would have us be? By the yardstick of heaven we are all deficient in some measure. However, a true Christian is one who is striving for these things. By the grace of God and the 'anointing from the Holy one' we show a longing for these things to be true of us. Meanwhile we take great comfort in 1 John 1:5–2:2. We must also bring ourselves under the tests John outlines in his first epistle with sincerity, resolve and humility, seeking God's forgiveness when sin is revealed. Before we throw a stone at another, we must examine ourselves.

Where there is an outright denial of the truth, a brazen rejection of the revealed way, our responsibility is quite plain: '"Everyone who confesses the name of the Lord must turn away from wickedness"' (2 Tim 2:19). When we are then charged with dividing the body of Christ, being schismatic or whatever, we must point out that it is not we who 'divide the seamless robe of Christ'. Jude 18–19 makes it very plain: '"In the last times there will be scoffers who will follow their own ungodly desires." These are the men who divide you, who follow mere natural instincts and do not have the Spirit.' The scoffers are the dividers – those who in following their own ungodly desires have themselves collected disciples around them.

Sometimes the denial of the truth is rationally argued and apparently reasonable. It is more reasonable to reject the miraculous than to accept it; more popular to say it does not matter either way. John Whale, who has the crucially important position of Head of BBC religious television, epitomised this position in an article in *The Sunday Times* on Easter Day 1986. Writing about the reaction caused by 'the driving honesty' of the Bishop of Durham, he went on to report on the Archbishop of Canterbury presiding over a meeting of bishops at Lambeth whose task was to 'approve a new firm statement of Church of England orthodoxy':

> It is unlikely to restore doctrinal discipline. Believers are of many different dispositions: they will continue to choose those forms of belief that they find persuasive. It is entirely possible to find solace and example in a Jesus of normal human birth, but of a religious genius which gives him a relation with God never paralleled before or since.
>
> The facts of Jesus' trial and death are well enough attested. There are Christians who find themselves more helped by the thought that a mere man bore those griefs as he did than that a man who was also God bore them.
>
> Similarly, it is clear enough that, after the first Easter, Jesus' followers showed remarkable faith and fortitude. Was that because they had witnessed a miraculous resurrection, or because they fed in their hearts on his message and came to see that it was still with them? There are Christians who take more encouragement from the second explanation than the first.

Of course the miraculous account of events is not to be ruled out. But neither is the non-miraculous. Events that have proved of such stupendous importance, governing millions of lives, must retain an element of mystery. Certainty in these things is attractive, but not attainable.

We cannot align ourselves with such thinking. It is not a matter of take it or leave it, of which option suits you best. To deny the resurrection is to deny Christ. We dare not renege from this position. It is those who, in divorcing themselves from the revealed faith and in their rejection of the Saviour, have failed the test of John in his first epistle and are not to be counted among those 'who know'.

Elsewhere the Bible seems to make it clear that there is a separation that cannot be accomplished now by men but which must wait for the Last Day when God himself will perform the task. Jesus referred to this in the parable of the weeds (Mt 13:24–30) and the parable of the net (Mt 13:47–52).

Dr Peter Masters confronts this exegesis in the booklet *Separation and Obedience*. First, he poses the argument of those who would say that we must not divide now but leave the matter to the subsequent activity of God:

> It is our duty to stay in denominations no matter how bad they become, and also to co-operate in our evangelism with those who do not share evangelical views, because the Lord tells us that His Church is bound to contain good and bad elements until the Day of Judgement. The parable of the wheat and tares tells us not to attempt to secure a pure Church, but to let both grow together until the harvest.

and then we have his answer:

> Those who use this argument in favour of inclusivism do not take account of the Lord's own interpretation of His parable. They

57

seem to think that the *field* in which the wheat and tares grow together represents *the Church*. They therefore conclude that the parable is talking about the Church when it says that Christians and unsaved people will exist together until the harvest.

However the Lord tells us in Matthew 13:38 that the field represents *the world*, not the Church! The parable does not speak about the Church at all.

This elementary mistake in exposition of the parable has led to teaching which contradicts numerous New Testament passages. Verse after verse calls us to watch for false teaching, to keep it out of our congregations, and to reject those who are responsible for it.[8]

Now that is a fair comment. But Masters does not deal with the net in the second parable. Commentators say that whereas quite clearly the teaching on the parable of the net is fundamentally the same as the parable of the weeds, the net cannot be the world. Of course, there is a terrible danger of applying a parable too specifically at any one point to the exclusion of the whole. Nevertheless, the net is not the world – the lake is the world. It is the gospel that catches men (Lk 5:10).

William Hendriksen in his commentary on Matthew says of this parable:

> However, not all of those that enter the kingdom in its visible manifestation – for all practical purposes we might as well say not all those who enter the church visible – are truly saved. This will become evident in the great day of judgment when the angels will separate the wicked from the righteous.

This is confirmed in the Baptist Confession of 1689, paragraph 26.3:

> The purest churches under heaven are subject to (liable to be affected by) mixture and error,[1] and some have degenerated so

much that they have ceased to be churches of Christ and become synagogues of Satan.[2] Nevertheless Christ always has had, and always will (to the end of time) have a kingdom in this world, made up of those who believe in Him, and make profession of His name (witness for Him).[3]

1. 1 Cor. 5; Rev. 2 & 3.
2. Rev. 18:2; 2 Thess. 2:11–12.
3. Matt. 16:18; Ps. 72:17; Ps. 102:28; Rev. 12:17.

So if a pure church is impossible, does that mean that we are not expected to seek it and work for it? Of course not. In our local church fellowships we have just such a responsibility. It is a duty which should humble us, for like holiness, which is a command yet also an aspiration, we are constantly aware of our own sin and shortcomings. Separation will be on some cardinal issue, from some fundamental denial of truth, not as we have recently witnessed on such matters as 'second degree separation' which we will examine more closely later on.

Could we in truth remain with a church that condones sin, never seeks to deal with those who deny the fundamentals of the faith, turns a blind eye to outstanding error, never seeks to discipline those who are loveless in word or deed? How one and another work this out practically is between them and the Lord. But let none of us be overconfident that we are untinged by error or unsullied by compromise, for that is a form of pride which receives its come-uppance from the Saviour by the most implacable censure.

Pharisaism is a term of reproach today, and quite rightly so. We might think that the Pharisees were in serious doctrinal error to receive such a strident censure from the Saviour. Far from it. Their concern was to keep the law –they were model Jews (Phil 3:5–6). Their emphasis was on individual piety and strict ethical standards and the necessity of being separate from anything or anyone who might fall short of their own self-imposed standards. So why were they condemned rather than commended by Christ? It was because they were holier-than-thou, totally lacking in love and mercy. They did right in the letter of the law, but wrong in the spirit. Seeing that the Lord Jesus is unchanging, the pharisaical attitude must still be an affront to him and worthy of his rebuke.

How my heart goes out to the Apostle Paul – there was no arrogant self-satisfaction in him:

> It is true that some preach Christ out of envy and rivalry, but others out of good will. The latter do so in love, knowing that I am put here for the defence of the gospel. The former preach Christ out of selfish ambition, not sincerely, supposing that they can stir up trouble for me while I am in chains. But what does it matter? The important thing is that in every way, whether from false motives or true, Christ is preached. And because of this I rejoice (Phil 1:15–18).

Let me give you an illustration. Unfortunately there are times in a human marriage when the behaviour of one of the partners causes the other to leave the matrimonial home, even though that one loves their home. Yet they have a greater responsibility than keeping the home together; the welfare of the children is at stake. The separation is grievous but unavoidable. The step of leaving is a last resort entered into reluctantly. Nevertheless, the hope is for reconciliation and coming together on the terms of first love, first allegiance and repentance of the sin that caused the division. Sadly, pastors know of such things even in Christian marriages. It has been a heart-rendering matter but they have felt there to be no other alternative.

But there is also another type of separation. A wife is supportive and faithful, yet her husband tires of her. He wants something different, more exciting. The routine of home has become dull and predictable. Certain annoying habits and petty shortcomings are blown up out of all proportion. So he leaves. A separation takes place.

The first situation described, when every avenue has been explored, every genuine attempt has been made, all overtures rebuffed, is inevitable. The second situation is intolerable, outrageous and sinful.

It is the same with separation from the church. History reveals times when the faithful have been driven out, excommunicated, from the church. But division has also come about through petty foibles and squabbles, clashes of personality, selfish ambition and love of power. John remarks: 'They went out from us, but they did not really belong to us. For if they had belonged to us, they would have remained with us; but their going showed that none of them belonged to us' (1 Jn 2:19).

This verse appears in the context of final perseverance. It speaks of those who were in the visible church but never in the spiritual. Nevertheless, when people separate from us for reasons other than those laid down in Scripture, they reveal what sort of people they are. They show that they do not belong to us. When I hear of separation within a fellowship of churches unequivocal in its gospel stance, undiluted in its statement of faith, God-honoured in its witness to the world, for issues trite if not mistaken, spiteful if not vindictive, I wonder what sort of people these are. Time, of course, will tell. It has all happened before, as a cursory reading of the history of Evangelicalism will reveal. Some feel well able to judge, and usually do so; some are quick into print, ever ready to name names. But we will leave the matter with God. As Paul advised: 'Therefore judge nothing before the appointed time; wait till the Lord comes. He will bring to light what is hidden in darkness and will expose the motives of men's hearts. At that time each will receive his praise from God' (1 Cor 4:5). How desperately we need discernment in these matters. And this is promised:

But you have an anointing from the Holy One, and all of you know the truth (1 Jn 2:20).

As for you, the anointing you received from him remains in you, and you do not need anyone to teach you. But as his anointing teaches you about all things and as that anointing is real, not counterfeit – just as it has taught you, remain in him (1 Jn 2:27).

The word 'anointing' or 'unction' comes from the Greek word *chrisma* (not *charismata*). Its Hebrew equivalent is *messiah* and refers to the Old Testament practice of anointing with oil. It came to be associated with the setting apart or consecration to the Lord's work with oil. Sometimes this could be holy things for the temple worship, sometimes holy people such as Aaron and his sons. Eventually this anointing came to be linked with the coming of the Holy Spirit, as in the case of the anointing of Saul:

Then Samuel took a flask of oil and poured it on Saul's head and kissed him, saying, 'Has not the Lord anointed you leader over his inheritance?' (1 Sam 10:1).

The Spirit of the Lord will come upon you in power, and you will prophesy with them; and you will be changed into a different person (1 Sam 10:6).

and David:

So Samuel took the horn of oil and anointed him in the presence of his brothers, and from that day on the Spirit of the Lord came upon David in power (1 Sam 16:13).

Gradually the 'Anointed One', the Messiah, became the title for the One who was to come – *the* Messiah. '"Know and understand this: From the issuing of the decree to restore and rebuild Jerusalem until the Anointed One, the ruler, comes, there will be seven 'sevens', and sixty-two 'sevens'"' (Dan 9:25).

When in the love of God the Messiah came, born of the virgin Mary at Bethlehem, he was called in Greek *Christos*, 'the Anointed One'. The Holy Spirit descended upon him (Lk 3:22). And that was also his promise to the disciples: 'For John baptised with water, but in a few days you will be baptised with the Holy Spirit' (Acts 1:5). And what of those who received the promise?

Acts 11:26 tells us that 'the disciples were first called Christians at Antioch.' They were followers of the anointed one – or the anointed ones – those who had received the Holy Spirit.

John says to us: 'You have an anointing from the Holy One' (1 Jn 2:20). This is an anointing to know the truth. The liars are those who deny that Jesus is the Christ. We have a responsibility in this matter: 'See that what you have heard from the beginning remains in you. If it does, you also will remain in the Son and in the Father' (1 Jn 2:24). And we have received a promise: 'And this is what he promised us – even eternal life' (1 Jn 2:25). Concerning 'those who are trying to lead you astray' (1 Jn 2:26), we have an anointing remaining in us, an anointing that is real that we might remain in him (1 Jn 2:27).

This anointing is for every child of God. It is not for knowing everything – that sadly cannot be – but for knowing the 'eternal gospel' in Christ by the Holy Spirit of truth. Jesus promised: 'And I will ask the Father, and he will give you another Counsellor to be with you for ever' (Jn 14:16). And John wrote: 'But you have an anointing from the Holy One, and all of you know the truth' (1 Jn 2:20). No Christian has ever been led into error by the Holy Spirit.

Any teaching or leading that denies the work of the Spirit in regard to the believer's standing in Christ (Rom 8:9–11), or his fellowship in the Spirit with all God's true children, whoever they be and wherever they be (Rom 8:12–16), or denies what God has done in Christ by his Spirit (1 Cor 12:12–13) in bringing us into one body, is not of the truth. We have an anointing to discern that and stand against it. By the Holy Spirit within us, we should know when someone is denying the fundamentals of the faith and resist this. Similarly, if another, under whatever name and from whatever lofty or plausible motive, is seeking to separate what God has brought together, there should be an 'inner witness' of the Spirit that this must not be.

More and more Bible Christians have become increasingly worried and deeply concerned about trends among us. There is rampant compromise on the one hand, and the setting up of new churches at a stroke on the other. Added to this, there is a growing isolationist group. Each feeds off the other and is the cause of the other. One, in reaction to cold legalism, tends to throw out the baby with the bath water and say that nothing matters as long as one's spirit is right. This only reinforces the separatists in their belief that the former are compromising, especially when they make statements that underline and confirm their fear. The others say 'A plague on all your houses' and opt out altogether.

I am sure that the Spirit of God has revealed another way – that an unction is given to 'children' who, because they have been born into the family of God cling to the family and love their brothers and sisters in Christ and wish to remain together in the Father's house. Families are built on trust. No child is the same either in gift or in attitude. We say to our own brothers and sisters in the faith, your way is not ours, we differ in that regard, but you are still the family and nothing can alter that. Everything that really matters we share in common; our hopes, fears and needs are the same. I reason with you as a brother. I seek to explain my understanding as a brother. Here and there we agree to differ – as brothers. But nothing will be allowed to break up the home.

5

Some Present-Day Clichés

This book is about Evangelical unity. It is addressed to Evangelicals who subscribe to the historic understanding of the word of God as that body of biblical teaching generally described as primary truth. Now among such, those whose only authority is what the Bible says, there are obviously divisions. Some, like myself, are to be found in the historic mixed denominations. Some consider such denominations to be outside the purpose of God and beyond the possibility of fellowship, and move in areas of independency. Still others feel both groupings to be largely irrelevant to what God is doing today and have formed new constituencies under the general heading of Renewal.

Among the first two there are three phrases which are prevalent, 'in it to win it', 'guilt by association', and 'second degree separation'. They are used either to attack the one position or the other, and I want to look at them in some detail for they are crucial to understanding the present malaise and must be faced if there is any hope of progress in Evangelical unity.

1. In it to win it

Among those ministering among the historic denominations,

the phrase 'in it to win it' has been used to justify working in a denomination where there are both Evangelicals and those who would never make any claim to be so. You might feel from what has been said above that I would support the argument of a man who says, 'I will go to a dead church as its minister to win it back for the gospel. I will join a local church with my family to be a witness to the truth. I will throw my weight into the councils and committees of my denomination as a witness to the gospel.' You would be both right and wrong. I believe that such an argument is theologically suspect and pragmatically unsound. I defend my position from a different premise.

Let us look at this matter more closely in the light of 2 Corinthians 6:14–17:

> Do not be yoked together with unbelievers. For what do righteousness and wickedness have in common? Or what fellowship can light have with darkness? What harmony is there between Christ and Belial? What does a believer have in common with an unbeliever? What agreement is there between the temple of God and idols? For we are the temple of the living God. As God has said: 'I will live with them and walk among them, and I will be their God, and they will be my people.'

This vital portion of Scripture has been applied almost exclusively to the matter of a Christian marrying a non-Christian. This has served to push it into a very small drawer where it is put away and conveniently forgotten. But what of its wider application?

Geoffrey B. Wilson in his most helpful commentary on 2 Corinthians (Edinburgh, Banner of Truth, 1979) brings together some of the relevant statements of other writers on these verses:

> Lenski says, 'What business has he (the believer) in such an unnatural, self-contradictory association? What is he, the

believer, doing by helping to pull the plough or the wagon of the unbeliever's unbelief?'

Charles Hodge, 'Christians to remain Christian and retain their inward state as such, and yet to enter voluntarily into intimate fellowship with the world, is as impossible as to combine light and darkness, holiness and sin, happiness and misery.'

Matthew Poole, 'Christ has no fellowship with the devil, therefore we ought to have no unnecessary communion with such who manifest themselves to be of their father the devil by doing his work.'[9]

P.E. Hughes is also quoted, and his observation should be borne in mind in this crucial debate:

> 'What does a believer have in common with an unbeliever?' must not be interpreted as though it encouraged pharisaic concepts of contamination, or invited to eremitic (living alone in seclusion) and monastic attempts at segregation from 'the world'.
>
> In the Scriptures, 'the world', when not used in its literal sense, is 'the sphere and scene of human intercourse conditioned by our mortal and "natural" state', or 'a society, a system of sin-tainted humanity, not ruled by the love of God, not subject to His Son'.[10]

Now, quite clearly we are in the world to win it. Jesus said: 'My prayer is not that you take them out of the world but that you protect them from the evil one. They are not of the world, even as I am not of it. Sanctify them by the truth; your word is truth. As you sent me into the world, I have sent them into the world' (Jn 17:15–18). But in the popular use of the phrase 'in it to win it' more complex forces come into play.

Who uses this phrase? Let me try to illustrate by some hypothetical examples. First, a man fresh from theological college is seeking placement in his first church. He has been called by God, undergone some training, and has been set apart for the work of the ministry. He could encounter a variety of situations. His first pastorate could be among believers who have been led by God to found a ministry, have set spiritual parameters within which they work, and are now needing and looking towards an under-shepherd to lead them on in the word of God. To minister to such a group is as great a privilege as can be imagined. Their historical associations, or lack of them, are of little interest. There the minister can mature spiritually and be faithful to his calling.

On the other hand, he may find himself in an inner-city situation, among a dispirited people totally frustrated by the insufferable burden of maintaining vast decaying buildings let alone the social and ethnic needs and the dangers of the surrounding area. Then again, he might be called to the country, and so on. Wherever, the young minister will find giants of faith, babes in Christ, mixed outlooks, theological confusion if not ignorance, conflicting pressures in the areas of charismatic and Reformed, separation and denominationalism. He will meet all these situations, by the love and grace of God, with patience, tact and firmness. He will endeavour to lead his people to spiritual discernment and Christian maturity by the regular, relevant ministry of the truth. The title they hold, the details of history that brought about their affiliation would hardly been seen as a priority issue in such a calling. He sees a great opportunity and tries to meet it.

But there is another possibility that this man may be called to a situation that is not only spiritually dead but actively antagonistic to his biblical stance. A close friend of mine left college with me to just such a calling. Our prayer was that his people, coming to love their pastor would come to love his Lord. But we were wrong. There was antagonism to the preaching of the gospel, downright denial of the personal return of Christ, and distinct hostility to anything humanly unpalatable, such as the blood of Christ. The inevitable parting of the ways focused on the question of selling alcohol at the annual bazaar! What had taken place, rather than being a demonstration of Evangelical unity had been an unequal yoking together.

My friend, freed from the above situation, has gone on to be used most profitably in the kingdom of God. But the lesson is clear, no one must go against the word of God by entering a situation where he will be hindered in preaching the whole counsel of God. That the Bible forbids. That is being unequally yoked. But still, it is not a matter of denominationalism *per se*. That is not the primary consideration. Much better, I feel, to go to a pioneer situation and start from nothing than try to build on a foundation of sand. Unless we have the Rock that is Christ on which to build, nothing of lasting value can be constructed.

Closely related to the above is the apparently logical argument that goes something like this. My local church is dead, yet it seems wrong to travel three miles to the nearest gospel church. Therefore, my family will join this local fellowship to be light in the darkness, salt to the earth, yeast to the lump (and any other biblical metaphor you can think of). But this argument is wrong, desperately dangerous, and certainly unbiblical. Are you prepared to sit week after week under a ministry that is at best bland and of no consequence, and at worst an implicit or explicit denial of the person and work of Christ? Because if you are, then you are encouraging deceit, and you will be so continually a sore thumb, so continually at loggerheads with the leadership as to make the future untenable. Or again, are you prepared to allow your young children to be taught about the Christian faith in a Sunday school run by unbelievers, or let your teenagers be starved of Christian teaching and encouraged in a lifestyle contrary to what the Bible says? If the need of a local community without any gospel witness is laid heavily upon you, it is far better to begin a weekly meeting in a home, seek to share the burden with other Christians, and see if, by the grace of God, a foothold can be gained in that locality for the gospel. After all, this was almost undoubtedly the way that the 'dead' church had begun. I have no doubt that its foundation was in men and women of God seeking to raise a standard in the community to the claims of Christ. That the original vision waxed dim, subsequently to fade completely, shows the heavy responsibility that we have to those who have gone before us to ensure the continuance of the ministry of truth. Again, the label on the notice board or the historic denominational link is not the issue, but rather if the Spirit of God is still at work within the church.

In considering whether a church is 'dead' or 'alive', we must be very careful. Let me illustrate this from Scripture. Look at the letters to the seven churches of Asia in the book of Revelation. What contact would the separatists have with the majority of them? But the Lord brings no injunction for the people to leave those churches, and what a hotchpotch they are. Sardis is actually described as 'dead' (Rev 3:1), yet far from leaving it and condemning it to the fire, the Lord commands them to 'strengthen what remains' (Rev 3:2). Read the passage again for yourself – it is most thought provoking.

Sardis is accused of no heresy. In fact, outwardly it was a lively gospel church. But in effect the people had died in that they were not practising what they preached. They were to remember what they had received and heard in order to obey it. Like many churches where lofty doctrines are preached and high-faluting sentiments expressed, it had ceased to have any practical consequence. It had to repent of this sin. Added to this, there was a group of precious souls in the church who had not fallen asleep like the rest and were unsoiled from the sin of pietism without practice, orthodoxy without life. What was needed at Sardis was strengthening, not breaking down. It was not a 'dead' church.

Yet these letters also make it clear that false teaching is not to be tolerated. For Ephesus even to lose its first love is to court the danger of having the Lord 'come to you and remove your lampstand from its place' (Rev 2:5). Pergamum, theologically and morally compromised, is commanded to repent or else the Lord will soon come (Rev 2:16). Thyatira (Rev 2:18–29) is not to tolerate the woman Jezebel for the sake of unity; in fact, the church is to have nothing to do with her but to 'hold on' until the Lord comes. From the words to the church at Laodicea comes the most direct confirmation that false teaching is to be avoided. If the offence of being 'lukewarm' is sufficient for being spat out of the mouth of the Saviour (Rev 3:16), then what must be the fate of those who deny his name, decry his work, and ignore his word? It is too awful to think about. In its own estimation, the church at Laodicea was at the height of its spiritual and temporal success, yet the Lord vainly stood at the door knocking to come in. He loves the church and therefore rebukes it and disciplines it. So what is his attitude to that place destitute of the gospel, antagonistic to the cross? Would you wish to be part of it, to claim that the Lord had told you to go in when he has remained clearly outside? In the light of the above, we must be very careful about labelling a church as 'dead' or 'alive'. The number of times I have heard people describing a particular church as 'dead' is quite frightening. That the worship is formal does not mean that that church is dead. That it consists of a few aged and depressed souls who have maintained a witness at great cost and personal sacrifice does not mean it is dead. How careful we must be. Plainly, none of the seven churches referred to above was dead. The word is used far too carelessly today. What some mean is that a particular church is not charismatic, or it is not Reformed, or it is a member of a mixed denomination. They may actually be saying that the local church is not as they would like it, but that is something completely different. If we look at the other two churches out of the seven to which John wrote, Smyrna and Philadelphia, we see that neither would rank high on a list of popular or successful churches.

71

Smyrna (Rev 2:8–11) is persecuted and poor. No doubt there was little outwardly to attract and much to repel. Probably meeting 'down-town', they knew direct opposition for which the members suffered greatly. No swish programme, no system of organisations meeting the needs of every possible section and interest, no great music and probably no great congregation (I think real persecution would reduce many present-day congregations). Yet the Lord says of this church, 'I know' (Rev 2:9) – I understand. For Smyrna there is the long-term promise still sung at many baptisms: 'Be faithful, even to the point of death, and I will give you the crown of life' (Rev 2:10). To deny this church is to deny God. So that local group, fighting against horrible odds, depressed by opposition, disheartened by little visible encouragement, unable to maintain a large programme, without an organist or even an organ, unable to afford the support of a pastor, may not be dead but rather the apple of the Lord's eye and in the centre of his protecting care. Rather Smyrna than Laodicea any day. But we live at a time when the one is dismissed and the other exalted.

And as for Philadelphia (Rev 3:7–13), here again is a church with 'little strength' but with vast opportunity. The people have fulfilled the supreme responsibility of any worshipping fellowship, they have 'kept my word and have not denied my name' (Rev 3:8). It must be very hurtful for a church to be described as 'dead' when it has 'an open door', a vast area of responsibility, and is in desperate need of help. The Saviour says to it, 'Hold on to what you have, so that no-one will take your crown' (Rev 3:11).

In our ignorance we often make judgemental statements about other churches, quite unaware of the real situation. Certainly one is able to point to excesses in this area or that, contractions here and there, but is Jesus Christ owned as Lord? Is his saving claim made known and his saving power demonstrated? If so, however inadequately, dare you call it dead? If Christ is in a church to win it to himself, who are we to deny that work – or the faithful people who are striving alongside their Lord?

In the mixed denominations many men preach the whole counsel of God in areas of much discouragement. To dismiss them with a platitude is arrogant and ungodly. It is with God that they have to do, and with these diligent men he is evidently pleased to work. Beware lest you criticise the Almighty.

That local fellowship may not be dead at all. Dispirited, yes, facing terrible social problems, deprived of regular biblical ministry – but where, as at Sardis, there are 'a few people ... who have not soiled their clothes' (Rev 3:4), be careful before you dismiss them, for the living Christ will be at work among them. The denomination of such people is of little or no consequence. They are fighting for their very existence, not matters of ecclesiastical politics. Quite rightly, they have no time for that.

But if they are very clearly dead, if there is no desire to guard the pulpit from error, no visible hunger after righteousness, evidently no concern for the lost nor exercise of church discipline, then to join them – whoever they are, whatever the name they bear – is compromise, and compromise in the things of God is sin.

So what of the 'in it to win it' argument? The simple yet complex answer is that it depends on whom you are talking about. Again, you might imagine that as an accredited minister of a mainline denomination, it is a viewpoint I would defend unreservedly. But you would be wrong. The 'in it to win it' mentality, in its usual meaning, is both naïve and pretentious. It is naïve and wrong because we were never told by the Master to 'go and win denominations', but rather to 'go and make disciples'. Not to 'go into all the world to save structures and groupings', but to 'go into all the world and preach the gospel'.

A man goes into the ministry because he feels the irresistible call of God. Because he has a deep burden for the lost. Because he sees the real need for the people of God to be built up by the regular ministry of the word. He enters the ministry because he can do no other; the souls of men is his only concern. A man who feels it his calling and responsibility to win a denomination for Christ is certainly misguided and probably proud. Who is he to do such a thing? In my limited knowledge I have heard of some forming new denominations – 'The Wesleys', for instance – as an unsought for, unintended addendum to their God-given ministry. I have never heard of a man winning a denomination. Evangelicals ministering within denominations should have no ulterior motive than the glory of God and the extension of his kingdom. Everything else is secondary to that.

Surely we should thank God for men who stand for truth in high places; who, at the centre of ecclesiastical power, maintain a witness to the whole gospel? I would not be so sceptical as to question where they are. I am concerned about the sort of people they are. So many of the troubles within the denominations have been caused by seeking the middle way, the lowest common denominator. The need to be all-embracing, keeping two wings together. Failing to stand for truth lest it cause offence. Bland generalities to please most and offend few. How easy it is to be drawn into the general platitudes prevalent among such groups. If a man is going to operate here for Christ, he is often going to be lonely, under constant attack, ever threatened by compromise, resistant to being muted for 'the good of the whole'. Would such an uncompromised man be appointed or elected to high denominational office by his fellows? There are a few, but only a few. And if such a man believes himself called, and by the Spirit is equipped for such a ministry, then I thank God for him and will pray for him and stand with him. But for most of us our one concern is our ministry, our responsibility as under-shepherds of the flock of Christ. Everything else is secondary to that.

Many Evangelicals in mixed denominations are grateful to their theological colleges and feel a debt of love towards them. They appreciate those who maintain their denominational structures, for this has given them the training and opportunity to fulfil their calling which is no more and no less than any other minister of the gospel, namely seeking to make the claims of Christ known to the world. Which leads immediately into the next matter....

2. Guilt by association

The argument for 'guilt by association' goes something like this. As I am an accredited minister of a denomination that contains other accredited ministers who deny the fundamentals of the faith, I am implicated in their heresy because of the 'fellowship' I have with them.

Now, this argument is not to be dismissed at a stroke. For many it has led to seceding from their denominations at great personal cost and for others, who have remained, much soul searching. The theological issues have been examined in a previous chapter and I ask you to bring them to bear here. I do not want to criticise those who have separated nor condone those who have stayed in. My plea is that Evangelical unity must embrace all those who have been 'honest to God' about the position they hold in the light of God's word and for the consequences of this. Another person's action or lack of it may not be mine, but I will trust that he, like me, has examined his heart and mind in the light of God's word and has come accordingly to the position he now holds. I do not speak of the Vicars of Bray among us who are all things to all men, and are blown by every puff, let alone wind, of doctrine. Much of today's distrust and conflict has been engendered by such men who change their platform at a stroke.

No, we must hold consistently to the position we have reached under God, for then we know whom we're dealing with, and have a degree of certainty that they are the same people today as those we spoke to yesterday.

Let me point to personal experience to explain what has moulded my thinking. As a young man brought up in a fine Evangelical baptist church in loose membership of the Baptist Union, sensing the call of God to the ministry I was first directed to an independent Bible college. The principal of that college subsequently encouraged me to go to Spurgeon's College where I spent three challenging, happy and altogether rewarding years. The events of 1966 – the Dr Martyn Lloyd-Jones/John Stott debate, such a watershed for many – were not known to me. Sundays not preaching were spent at Westminster Chapel where I thrilled to the exposition of God's word. After my course I freely and gladly signed the Baptist Union basis of faith, believing that my colleagues would also sign in good faith. At the same time, bearing in mind that a great deal of money had been invested by others in my training, I committed myself in writing to serving at least three years within the Baptist Union. Soon after ordination and within my probationary period, Michael Taylor at the Baptist Union annual assembly clearly and unequivocally denied the deity of Christ. Not only did I deplore that, but I felt guilty and in some way implicated by it. I do not speak for others; this is a strictly personal statement. At that time I was both legally and morally bound to the Union; I could h ave no thought of leaving. I was heartened by the costly stand that the principal of Spurgeon's College made in defence of the gospel. During this period I was pastor of a church where God was at work in undeniable blessing, and I threw all my energies into that.

Meanwhile I was deeply involved at committee level with the Baptist Revival Fellowship, at that time very much the meeting place for conservatives in the Baptist Union who

were also grappling with the issues mentioned above. Some
had succeeded, some had not. Almost immediately after
being accepted onto the accredited list at the close of my
probationary period, I accepted a call to a church in Bournemouth absolutely united in the gospel and loosely linked to
the Baptist Union – so loosely that the average member both
then and now would not have known that the church had any
such affiliation at all. Here again the question of association
came up. I decided that whatever happened, pastor and
people would move together.

The lovely building in which we met was only a few years
old. It had been built with the help of Baptist funds; the
church was tied by the famous or infamous 'Model Trust
Deed'. Once again I was faced with an imponderable problem, ethical as well as strictly theological. Money had been
lent in good faith by people of goodwill. It had been an
investment in the gospel showing obvious dividends for the
kingdom of God. It was clear that God was demonstrating his
ongoing purposes among us. Would he be glorified by the
inevitable court action and possible legal wranglings that
would follow after such a recent loan of money both given
and received in good faith? No, rather than feeling
antagonistic to those who had made these funds available, we
felt genuine gratitude. Their generous help had been clearly
recognised by God. Whether, if I had been minister at the
time of rebuilding, I would have looked to this source for
help is not the point. Quite clearly, God had not withdrawn
his mandate from us.

Then came another change of circumstance. Feeling the
call of God to my last church, an independent Baptist church
in fellowship with Strict Baptists, the way seemed clear: I
would resign from the accredited list of the Baptist Union.
Added to this, I received a letter from the Baptist Union saying that since I had taken a pastorate in another grouping
I was being removed from the denominational list of

accredited ministers. But five things happened that changed that situation.

First, I discovered that the Strict Baptist statement of faith and order had a 'closed communion table' clause that in all conscience I could not and would not sign. If I had felt free to sign, that would have been the end of the matter as far as my being accredited to the Baptist Union, but I needed to feel in ministerial fellowship with someone. Secondly, my new deacons, knowing prior to my acceptance of the call to that church of my theological dilemma with regard to the communion table, unitedly asked me not to take any hasty action in leaving the Baptist Union as they were anxious that no step should be made that would apparently leave me in full fellowship with no one. Unable to enter into association with the Strict Baptists, I agreed to respect these wishes for a period. Thirdly, a certain degree of reaction was expressed even by the area superintendent over the intention to remove my name. He believed that I represented a stance needed in the Union, and that this influence would be weakened by my removal. The Ministry department of the Baptist Union reconsidered its position and agreed that my name could remain on the list. Fourthly, I was becoming very worried about the separatist trends within some parts of independent Evangelicalism, and I didn't want to take any definite action until my thinking was formulated and my conscience clear before God and man. Fifthly, since then, even during the course of writing this book, I have once again been called to a church in membership with the Baptist Union. Duke Street's only consideration was whether I was the man God had led to the pastorate, irrespective of my accreditation or otherwise to the Baptist Union.

When a man joins any denomination he usually endorses by signature that group's theological basis. He asks himself three questions: (1) Is the statement which he signs biblical truth? (2) Is it sufficiently full? (3) Is it entered into in good faith? The first question is the most important one, but it is not conclusive, for most if not all of my readers could gladly consent to the articles of the World Council of Churches. Secondly, only the Church of England of the major denominations would have a statement in any sense comprehensive and binding, namely the thirty-nine articles. And thirdly, as has been said by another recently, one can only presume that the majority consent to these credal statements 'with their fingers crossed behind their backs'.

From the above we can see that each one of us is personally responsible for our actions and will have to give individual account before the judgement seat of Christ. In that regard I am not my brother's keeper. If, for instance, a minister of the FIEC denies his statement of faith, this does not make all the other ministers guilty. However, they do have a responsibility to remonstrate with that wayward brother, either to win him back to his first love or to discipline him and subsequently, if there is no change of mind, to seek to remove him. What a man believes is between him and God; no one can be forced to assent to anything. But if of his own free will he signs a statement of faith, then he should abide by it and be honourable enough to resign if his position becomes untenable.

But suppose that the man will neither recant nor resign, saying that he does believe in the statement but in a way not commonly understood, or that the statement is an anachronism and not binding. Certain things must be obvious. First, this man is a cheat and a troubler of the churches, and must be treated as such. Secondly, the whole of the structures should not, nor could not, be disbanded because of that one man. Thirdly, it is futile and ridiculous to declare that all are guilty because of the behaviour of this one. What would make the position untenable would be if the basis of faith was adjusted to accommodate this man, the ground rules changed for his benefit.

When a man enters a mixed denomination with deep sincerity, signs a biblical statement of faith, and seeks to uphold it in thought, word and deed, and another – or probably several – do so carelessly or even flippantly for their own selfish purposes, he and his colleagues must remonstrate with them, they must bring pressure upon their denominational heads to uphold the truth and safeguard the denomination. There is no comfort or merit in being a broad church, as some imply, nothing advantageous in being on 'the Evangelical wing' of a mixed denomination, for there are frustrations and sorrows all down the line. Spurgeon was prophetic not only for Baptists in his insight during the 'Downgrade Controversy'. Men of faith at that time failed the truth and opened the floodgates of compromise by no doubt well-intentioned, fraternal desire to be all-embracing. And what could be said of Baptists could be said of all other denominations.

So, then, a man who enters a denomination in good faith, abides by the promises he has made, holds to the statements to which he has assented, is not implicated in the guilt of the cheater and the compromised in that denomination. A man will be 'guilty by association' only if he condones plurality of faith, runs with the hare and the hounds, seeks to be all things to all men, and blandly holds to his Evangelical faith without any regard to its practical consequences in standing up against error and darkness. But if this same man, under a strong call from God, takes a denominational church as an opportunity for the gospel, is faithful first and foremost in his God-ordained work there, and disassociates himself from that which he believes to be unworthy, he will certainly not be 'guilty'. Rather, he will be fulfilling his calling from God to exercise a costly and strategic ministry. He will often be an unpopular bedfellow yet, as has been evidenced time and time again, he will be singularly blessed.

So much of the separatist debate has been about the under-shepherds of the sheep. But what of the sheep themselves?

When the Saviour commanded his disciples to 'go into all the world and preach the gospel', there was no proviso 'save to those in mixed denominations'. They, too, need to hear. There are literally thousands who will blossom and grow under a biblical ministry, hundreds of churches that want nothing more or less than a full-orbed gospel ministry and will take a lead from a warm man of firm conviction. When such a man is called and used, we should rejoice. Rather than censure him, let us do all within our power to encourage and uphold him in prayer. Such a man is guilty of nothing, but rather obedient to his heavenly calling.

It is strange that I have found it easier to be consistent for the truth as I understand it within denominationalism than I have within separatist circles. In the former there has often been warm friendship and constructive support at best, and benign indifference at worst. In the latter, at best the peace and joy that comes from being with brethren of like mind and experience, and at worst downright coldness and hostility. It is strange that those who profess most, who have the letter of the matter, can so often miss the spirit. It is ridiculous and offensive to say that I am guilty because I have associated with a man I have never heard, would not recognise by sight, who would never be allowed into my pulpit, and whose views if I ever heard them would be an anathema to me. But I would be guilty if I were to acquiesce or even condone this man's right to continue to minister in flagrant disregard of the basis on which he was accepted. A man is guilty if he is one thing in one place and another in another. You cannot have it both ways. There are brave men of deep conviction within the same denomination as one with whom they can have no fellowship, who denies the central truths of the gospel, and even the Lord Jesus himself. In the case of Baptist churches, they are independent. Nothing can be impinged upon them from outside; they are totally free as to what denominational contribution they make or otherwise.

One last thing. And this is a valid if controversial question. The issues have been known and debated long enough now to ask what God's verdict has been on this matter. Have churches come under the continuing judgement of God? Some churches, when they have been disobedient to the truth, have deflected from the way, but others are knowing monumental blessing. There are also churches very close to me who have succeeded at great cost but not with great blessing. Blessing is not, of course, the criterion. We are not obedient to gain 'reward'. But nevertheless, is there undeniable evidence that God is at work among our 'separatist' brethren in some unique way indicative of a special relationship? I simply ask the question. What I do know is this. That if a man – whoever he is, wherever he is – is born again of the Spirit of God, knows the unction of that same Spirit, and ministers the word of life, there will be signs following. Perhaps Almighty God is less sensitive as to with whom he will associate than some of his disciples!

3. Second degree separation

This phrase, much in use and heatedly debated, is mainly a product of the last few years. Dr Peter Masters, who openly supports the teaching and in large measure has brought it to the attention of Evangelicals, asks the following questions in his booklet *Separation and Obedience*:

> Should we separate from Evangelicals who wilfully and enthusiastically fellowship and co-operate with false teachers such as liberals and Catholics? Many Evangelicals who themselves maintain biblical separation from those who repudiate the true gospel are perplexed about how they should regard other Evangelicals who go out of their way to co-operate with these false teachers. Should they break fellowship with them as well? Is what is called 'secondary separation' right or wrong?[11]

Under *this* definition, secondary separation is undoubtedly right, and all true Bible Christians would understand it
to be so. How can one have fellowship based on trust with a
man who says he is an Evangelical and yet 'wilfully and
enthusiastically fellowships and co-operates with false
teachers such as liberals and Catholics'? The matter is quite
clear, the faithful believer must separate from such people,
in so far as they teach false doctrine.

If you object that this statement contradicts what has just
been said above, then you have misunderstood me. A pastor
in a mixed denomination is not to take a lesser view of truth;
rather he is to be *more* vigilant in guarding his fellowship and
maintaining his stance. He must be unequivocal and uncompromised before God and man. Being all things to all men
has never been the way of Christ. Dr Masters gives four per-
fectly valid reasons why this must be so:

(1) The one who co-operates deals a terrible blow to the
exclusive nature of the gospel.

(2) He helps the devil achieve one of his main objectives:
to cause such confusion that the world no longer sees a distinctive biblical Christianity standing clearly apart from
Catholic and liberal error.

(3) He lowers the guard of the people of God and exposes
them to the extreme danger of infiltration by false believers
and false doctrine.

(4) He encourages false teachers in their infidelity and sin,
and strengthens them in their work.

Now, I firmly believe that these arguments are irrefutable.
It has to be plainly yet lovingly explained why the wilfully
inconsistent brother is such a problem. The person who seeks
the best of both worlds, is chummy with all shades of theological opinion, and is happily at one with whatever group he
associates with at any moment, is an embarrassment to the
gospel. Any meaningful sharing in witness and ministry with
him is difficult.

Most of us can understand that, and yet there is a problem that has sprung from the 'secondary degree separation' debate which rather than strengthening Evangelical unity is fragmenting it further. We have touched on this matter already. Sadly, those who were close friends and confidants have become estranged, organisations such as the British Evangelical Council have come under great strain, tempers have been raised, and confidence damaged. And this has happened not between those who 'enthusiastically fellowship and co-operate with false teachers', but between those altogether faithful according to the light that they have received and in the place where they believe they have been put by God. The 'secondary degree separation' debate has led to mistrust of another's ministry, suspicion of a person's integrity before God, rumour and recrimination, and much unhappiness. Some who hold their position from the highest of motives have been 'characterised and deliberately misunderstood' and their very integrity before God has been attacked. Still others, who in obedience to what they believe to be the purposes of God have stood against association, have equally suffered. It is a very sad state of affairs.

The matter was highlighted and intensified by a meeting of separatist ministers at Hinckley and subsequently at Rugby. Clause 4 of their agreed basis reads:

> We declare our intense sorrow that some of our fellow ministers who affirm the same doctrinal truths nevertheless compromise them by failing to speak out against and separate themselves from those who deny these truths and undermine them. Such failure hinders our ability to stand together with these brethren for a clear witness to the truth.

Now, knowing some who are leaders of this group, I doubt whether it was their intention to cause the dismay that they undoubtedly have. I doubt whether this statement is all they wish to be known by. If they have gathered to 'stand together' for a clear witness to the truth, then we will look forward to its practical outworking with genuine hope and anticipation. Some among them have left their denomination at tremendous cost and are to be honoured. The whole thesis of this book is that a person who seeks Evangelical unity must be consistent, and many of these have been wholly consistent. But much sorrow and distrust has been engendered – either through lack of sensitivity to others, or lack of foresight as to the implications of their action or, worst of all, by lack of love. Can the cause of Christ truly be furthered if Evangelicalism is split yet again? Where does it end?

Passages that forbid compromise are plentiful and clear in Scripture, and we have already examined some of them. I cannot and will not believe that a bland, comprehensive church is a tenable one – in fact, it is to be resisted at every point. Yet is there a passage that explicitly and positively teaches that a person may separate from a brother in Christ or a gospel church consistent in its stand, honouring in its use of Scripture, bold in its affirmation of truth but having an association or structure not to that person's liking? The passage frequently quoted is 2 Thessalonians 3:6 – 'In the name of the Lord Jesus Christ, we command you, brothers, to keep away from every brother who is idle and does not live according to the teaching you received from us.' The apparent consequence of disobedience is given in verses 14–15 – 'If anyone does not obey our instruction in this letter, take special note of him. Do not associate with him, in order that he may feel ashamed. Yet do not regard him as an enemy, but warn him as a brother.'

That fellow Christians are being addressed is clear. They are idle and do not live according to the teaching they have received. The following verse makes it clear that there are spongers in the church, living off the endeavours of others.

They are commanded to work. If they are still disobedient, they are to be noted and association withdrawn so that they might feel condemned. If only these idle brothers had known what misery they would cause to Bible Christians in the twentieth century. Of course, in another context it could be an immoral brother or a bitter one or a covetous one or an ambitious one or a loveless one that comes under censure. Incidentally, if a lazy brother is to be dealt with so firmly, what about one who denies the person and work of Christ or some other crucial doctrine? Surely he must be dealt with all the more severely? But as I cannot believe that such a person is a brother in the Evangelical sense (he is an antichrist), then that situation is not being addressed here.

But what about the one who does 'live according to the teaching he has received', who before God and man is totally consistent with the truth he has been given? What then? If you withdraw from him you should be ashamed. For if this lazy Christian is not to be regarded as an enemy, then I certainly should not consider my brother, who for whatever reason seems to be fragmenting the body of Christ, as an enemy. I long for and will continue to seek fellowship with him wherever possible, but I will also warn him as a brother. He must be made to feel ashamed.

Those who know me best would agree that, however inadequately, I do endeavour to be consistent in whatever circumstances to the truth as I understand it from the word of God. What is needed today are people of conviction. Sadly for some of us, this consistency in conviction has been as costly in some conservative circles as it has been in liberal – and seeing that some of us *only* move in conservative circles, then more so. It is not only the separatists who have suffered for what they firmly believe to be the will and purposes of God.

6

The Relationship between Various Evangelical Groupings

If all those who would be happy to be called Evangelical, as I have described it, were to be gathered into one place, after the initial joy of meeting it would not be long before pressures would inevitably lead to fragmentation. 'All one in Christ Jesus' – but not for long! Countless things would mark the various groups. Those in the main-line denominations and independents. Anabaptists and paedobaptists. Those convinced of congregational government, the presbytery system and Episcopalians. Charismatics, Reformed and Arminian would, of course, form their own groups for fellowship and support. Various views of the Lord's return would certainly bring a degree of friction. The version of the Bible read and used has also become another area for emotive debate. What hymn book do you use? What instruments do you find acceptable for worship? And so we could go on. Was it ever intended to be like this? Of course not. All would agree that the situation is contrary to the mind of Christ. I have touched on only a fraction of the matters which divide us. Even groups meeting under an agreed statement of faith for a common purpose find themselves distressed by the fragmentation felt among them.

That there is a problem, none can deny. To perpetuate schism for its own sake, or for personal prestige or party gain, or from intolerance or refusal to try to listen to what someone else is saying is clearly sinful. To hide behind one's own labels and then to condemn another because of his is to deny our oneness in the body of Christ.

Unless the Holy Spirit does a gracious work among us, I can see no hope for the situation. To melt hearts of stone and make pliable minds as inflexible as pig iron will take a deep work of God. If I were a prophet in the limited sense of foretelling, I would say that this matter will continue to proliferate here, as in the United States, until biblical Christianity comes to know true persecution through the fire of tribulation. It is in the fire of adversity that secondary things will be seen for what they are, when the dross will be purified away. When the forces of light meet the forces of darkness, it will cast us wholly upon Christ and upon those who truly love the Saviour. The faint-hearted will have gone, the false will be shown for what they are, the spurious will cease to exist.

No one covets persecution, and the issue of Evangelical suspicion and recrimination is too serious and sad to wait till then. Are we to watch in helpless regret, too frightened or ashamed to speak out, or would God have us do something now?

In 1978 I spent a week at a theological college in the USA where the faculty and student body were delightful, the content of the teaching excellent, the hospitality very warm and generous. During a meal with the faculty, I innocently questioned some aspect of the pre-millennial view of the secret rapture. The response was so amazingly hostile that I thought I had inadvertently denied the virgin birth or the bodily resurrection of Christ! In Britain the reaction would probably not be so extreme on that issue, but there are plenty of others. How many of us have had a hostile confrontation over the use of the NIV (New International Version) rather than a 'proper' Bible? Or have been dismissed because of offending some on a secondary issue of sensitivity?

One of the primary causes of this problem is the use we make of labels. We seem to think that by tying a certain label around a man or group we can define him and then dismiss him. That we have explained a person away, pigeon-holed and forgotten him, or, worse, attacked him from ignorance, solves nothing. Most of the New Testament epistles are directed towards some vital issue: rectifying a problem, encouraging the wayward, rebuking the sinful, but never ever the denial of brotherhood or the refusal of fellowship with those who are in Christ. Problems are certainly faced but never despaired of. The church at Corinth is not written off as it would be today, but written to with patience, love and care. Discipline is certainly exercised but not excommunication.

Recently, a highly respected Evangelical newspaper has been literally torn in two – not for some heresy, shady dealing or suspect social behaviour, but rather because it refused to take one prescribed line on the entire subject of the charismatic movement, which led to the withdrawal of its financial backing. Look at many church bookstalls, or the paper-rack of any Bible bookshop, and you will find two papers rather than one – both with 'Evangelical' in their titles, both similar in type-face and format. How sad. The fragmentation goes on, both sides making their case. I am fully identified with the new Evangelical paper, yet all Christians of warm heart are saddened by what has occurred.

The attitude of so many Christians is that unless something represents their view, or conforms to their position, it is to be rejected. So a newspaper only has to give a bad review of a book coming from one section, or a good review of work emanating from a different camp (the paper did not write the review), or report an emphasis not their own, then by print and word the innuendos begin. Churches are placed in a terrible dilemma, one-time friends and contributors begin to distance themselves from one another, and calls for the removal of the offending parties are voiced. Yet is it not the responsibility of a Christian newspaper to report widely and to comment freely on the issues which its readership faces? The paper in question often took a different line from mine on the matter addressed in this book, but I did not reject it for that. In fact, I respected it the more because it was clearly in the pocket of none – until the holder of the purse-strings said enough is enough.

It is impossible to dismiss something or someone by a word, a cliché or a label. Labels can be dangerous; they always fall short of what they intend to do. Some of us who have been damaged by their careless use by others must in Christian charity also be careful how we use them. Has the word 'Evangelical' itself become a buzz word, a label declaring 'To be treated with care'? To describe oneself as an Evangelical has certainly become a flag of convenience for some. There is still a degree of kudos gained from its use. A whole host of people speaking and acting very differently from historic biblical Christianity, for reasons best known to them, wish to operate under the heading 'Evangelical'. We have often been embarrassed and compromised by what has ensued. But we dare not be robbed of this word. There must be Evangelical unity among those who stand in belief and practice without qualification on the fundamentals of the faith. Because of the emotive and political overtones of the American use of the word 'fundamentalist', some of us would wish to use that word with care, to define what we mean by it. Nevertheless, hold tight to the fundamentals we surely must.

In reaction to the misuse of labels, it has become fashionable to reject all of them. Ask such and such if he is an Evangelical and he will protest that he will not be pigeon-holed by man-made definitions. I, too, object to being pigeon-holed by others, but with Paul I would say, 'I am not ashamed of the gospel, because it is the power of God for the salvation of everyone who believes' (Rom 1:16). Let those who are 'not ashamed' stand, and stand consistently, on the word of God. Evangelical unity can only be fostered among those who are unequivocally Evangelical.

This leads me to reiterate yet again the closely related matter of honesty, for without it trust cannot be engendered. The point must be made again and again. Unless we consistently speak with the same voice, we belittle our calling and destroy our credibility. It is horribly possible to accommodate to whatever platform we find ourselves on and adapt to the constituency with which we are presently involved. It was a most painful experience to be audibly sighed against at a recent study conference on unity and separation. But it would have been more painful if I had denied what I believed to be true. Within a fortnight of this conference I was introduced in a televised interview by the statement 'You represent the Calvinists here?' before a largely charismatic constituency, but I was not ashamed of that either. For unless we endeavour to be consistently before men what we believe ourselves to be before God, what can be achieved? Accommodation is a natural weakness, and many are driven to silence by fear of men. But unity will grow when we know that the one with whom we have to do will not change with the wind or with the constituency with which he happens to be at any given moment.

Where there is honesty, trust can grow. And I have discovered that when I trust a person, love soon follows. Unless Evangelical unity springs from truth, honesty, trust and love, it will be but a cosmetic exercise, a papering over the cracks, and worse than useless.

Let us look at some of these labels.

Charismatic

Every reader should know that this is a scriptural word. It derives from the Greek word *charismata* meaning grace-gifts, and is found at several points in the New Testament. In its plural form it is linked to the extraordinary gifts of the Holy Spirit bestowed for some special ministry. We see this in Paul's words to Timothy: 'Do not neglect your gift, which was given you through a prophetic message when the body of elders laid their hands on you' (1 Tim 4:14). 'For this reason I remind you to fan into flame the gift of God, which is in you through the laying on of my hands' (2 Tim 1:6).

Now, ask the average church member what the word 'charismatic' means and he will be unable to tell you. Nevertheless, it has become a label for everything that is new, threatening and unpalatable to the one who uses it. If there is participation in worship, the use of Bible choruses, and the occasional raised hand, it is dismissed as the dreaded charismatic movement. The banality of the 'I am H.A.P.P.Y.' type of chorus is acceptable to this person, but the glory of 'He is Lord' is not. The doxology will be heartily sung – a four-line verse of praise to the triune God, but another doxology of equal merit, such as 'Majesty', will be rejected. Then there is the doubter who shakes his head and says, 'There is no cross in this praise' (a frequently heard criticism, and one that was probably justified in the past), oblivious to such precious pieces as 'The price is paid' and 'Led like a lamb', widely-used songs from the prophetic pen of Graham Kendrick and others.

Why do we dread our emotions or refuse to be demonstrative in worshipping the Saviour? Why sing 'His touch has still its ancient power', yet decry every apparent demonstration of that power? Why believe in the priesthood of all believers and yet curtail 'the work of the ministry' to the professional and specialist? Why only anticipate the blessing of God within the rigidity and therefore predictable safety of liturgical forms? If there is to be any unity across the charismatic divide, there must not only be contact but also the building up of trust and sensitivity.

How and where can contact be made? First, I feel, among leaders rather than through town-wide initiatives and events. Too often charismatics seem to imply that either the whole package is to be accepted or nothing. There are many who do not move in charismatic circles who are far from convinced by the exegesis of 1 Corinthians 13:8–12 that teaches that the 'gifts' were an authenticating sign to the Apostles and church prior to the coming perfection of Holy Scripture when they then ceased to be. But having said that, it does not mean that they are happy that banal repetitions of Biblical truisms are prophecy as the New Testament understands it. Nor that when specific foretelling takes place, its truth or otherwise is not verified but conveniently forgotten if unauthenticated. Nor that in areas of healing apart from the psychosomatic (and we thank God for those), there is so little verification at present when healing is claimed. Only a bitter, twisted personality would resent true acts of divine healing, therefore let them be seen and demonstrated that all might rejoice. But if continual instances of dramatic healing are reported without evidence, the folk story of the king's new clothes will be re-enacted in our day, with all the resulting disillusionment.

Then there is the musical element in charismatic worship. Some people have, by the grace of God, appropriated what is available to every believer by the Spirit of God yet really do find the continual noise irksome and the repetition counteractive to meaningful worship. Let me give a personal instance. My taste in music is classical. That is not to be priggish – it just happens to appeal to me. Therefore that obligatory group of lovely Christian young people with guitars, drums, synthesisers, etc., playing in a style suitable for Radio 2 and therefore appealing to the majority, does nothing for me. I love the words of some of the new songs and encourage my own young people to use their gifts in worship as above, but for me it does little – nor does it have to, because God has made us all different. I can take it in small doses, gladly enter into it from time to time, and do not stand against those for whom this style of musical worship is highly meaningful.

We are not all expected to be pressed into the same mould, for God's word is contrary to that. Evangelical unity does not place on us the necessity of accepting the whole package of another perspective and emphasis. 'I love you in the Lord but such and such is not for me' should not be seen as a breach of fellowship by the spiritually mature. I have no objection that some of the words in modern worship are simplistic. In our church we sing 'The greatest thing in all my life is loving you', followed by another two verses where the words 'serving you' and 'knowing you' are substituted. My usual reaction is, does it need three verses to say just three things, and how can all three be the 'greatest thing' without the other two being secondary?

Charles Wesley says more in one line than the above says ungrammatically in three repetitious verses. But to my dismay I have discovered that our young people find it difficult to understand what our great hymn writers are saying in every respect. Although we glory in lines of great theological truth such as, 'Our God contracted to a span, incomprehensibly made man,' they find it difficult to grasp such concentrated doctrine. Seeing that in each service I use at least three such masterpieces of inspired hymnology, surely love demands that I give them at least one opportunity to sing about truth in a way they can grasp easily and to a tune that appeals to them? No one is allowed to 'give and take' in regard to the fundamentals of the faith, but 'give and take' as to style and content of worship is a sign of spiritual maturity. No good is accomplished by quoting all the scare stories that are associated with the charismatic position. Neither is any good achieved by denying that some of the trends in certain groupings towards apostleship and authority make understanding and full unity even more difficult, if not impossible. But some of us feel it our responsibility before God to try.

Reformed

There is much misunderstanding in this position, from which to a degree I have suffered. 'Hyper-Calvinistic' is the first cliché to which those of a Reformed position are subject, thereby implying that such a person has no interest in the salvation of the lost or the preaching of the gospel to sinners. In fact, it is implied that the Calvinist's only interest beyond reading the puritans is conferences called to discuss the puritans. The Reformed are described as cold, clinical, doctrinaire and hard. Having pastored for over seven years a great church in association with Strict Baptists fully identifying with the Reformed emphasis, let me seek to put one or two things in perspective.

Although I have heard of hyper-Calvinists, I have yet to meet one. The churches I know are gospel churches feeling a deep responsibility to make known the grace of God. The pastors I have met have been men with a burden for the lost. Certainly I have been at conferences with men of hard faces and cold hearts, but they have been few. So what is the problem? Mistrust has led to mutual misunderstanding. To one the Reformed seem inflexible and unfraternal, while to the other the non-Reformed seem lax and compromised. Certainly there are caricatures of this position on both sides, but again most of the problems and misunderstandings arise from fear bred from lack of contact.

Try to understand this about the Reformed Christian. He works from certain precepts deeply implanted in his soul. That if salvation is of the Lord, then techniques and methods in evangelism can be at best suspect tools. That the biblical and time-honoured way of presenting Christ to the sinner is 'by the foolishness of preaching'. That what the Bible describes as sin is yet sin, and that as far as one is enabled the whole counsel of God is to be preached. But to say that Reformed people are uninterested in the gospel is a lie, and that they do not know encouragement or blessing in these days equally so.

Through the Reformed sector, truths have been recovered which are quite as dramatically important as any claims regarding the charismata. The emphasis of the sovereignty of God and the initiative of grace, the very bedrock of the faith, have been rediscovered and safeguarded. By their publishing houses and conferences a whole new generation of young men have been trained and established in churches where the full gospel is taught and applied with great profit.

But it works both ways. Let those with a Reformed emphasis understand and remember that God, both in history and today, has used and is using many outside their sector to do valiant work for the kingdom. We are not to count as unclean those whom God has saved and is using for his glory. Let Calvinists understand that the initiative of grace must imply that the sovereign God will himself take initiatives beyond their own capacity to understand, apart from their proscribed channels, though never in contradiction to himself. God works where and with whom he will, and it is not for us to argue.

Let those who are not of this persuasion also stretch out their arms to their Reformed brothers. Exclusive he might seem to be, unfraternal at times, but he may also be desperately lonely. He will certainly have some books of immense value to loan you, and the very gesture of fellowship mutually given and received will fulfil the command of Christ to 'love one another'.

Mixed denominations

Perhaps the most serious misunderstanding is in the area of fellowship with those in the main-line denominations. We have touched upon many of the issues in a previous chapter. Now I speak of the relationship between Evangelicals in the various groupings.

It seems often that Independents are totally ignorant of the pressures faced by faithful brothers in the main-line denominations. Again, those in the denominations are often so caught up with their own problems, structures and opportunities as to be thoughtless, even careless, of others outside. This is hardly right or honourable, but there are reasons for it. The Independent is rightly frightened by any hint of compromise of the truth. He has been taught constantly of the equivocal position of Evangelicals in the mixed denominations and is hesitant of contact and fellowship out of loyalty to God's word and from fear of what his peer group might say. The denominationalist, probably damaged by attitudes suffered before, having read much of what is said of him in certain publications, has become negative to Independents and will probably seek encouragement and fellowship from within his own groupings. But is God glorified in any of this? And is the cause of Evangelical unity furthered? Hardly.

Let the Independent Evangelical understand certain things. That the Evangelical in the mixed denomination is as desperately concerned at the trends as he – probably more so, for they impinge more closely upon him. That involvement with the structures of his denomination is only so far as they give him opportunity to minister Christ. That he is more than worried about the demands of central organisation over which he has little or no control yet which are costly in money, directed towards the status quo, and largely unrewarding. Remember that he, too, is grieved when one of his number denies the gospel, and desperately frustrated when links, often legal and binding, prohibit or frustrate his preferred course of action. But despite all this, in his fellowship he is seeing Christ at work, people being converted, members built up in the faith, the kingdom extended, and has a deep peace that he is in the place that God has put him.

But at the same time, this man is probably deeply hurt by the attitude of some of his brethren in other Evangelical groupings towards him. With all the will in the world he sees no obvious confirmation that God is working among them in some unique way, yet his presence at their conference seems to be an embarrassment, his overtures for fellowship politely spurned, his invitation for joint action in the gospel firmly resisted. No wonder positions are being entrenched and ever-higher barriers being raised. Yet each is a child of God called into the light, to be what God intends in witness to the world and brotherly fellowship with the faithful.

Under this heading I would make a special plea to Evangelicals within the Church of England, for there is a degree of confusion and uncertainty among those outside the established church for which they are not wholly responsible. Since Keele, and a decade later Nottingham, there seems among some Anglican Evangelicals not only a lack of interest in their free church brethren, but a positive seeking after unity with the Roman Catholic church that can only bring genuine disquiet to many. No one who holds to the sovereignty of God would deny that in his loving purposes there are converted men and women within the Roman Catholic church, but the seeking after visible unity with the church of Rome with which some Anglican Evangelicals are engaged seems to us to be either a dangerous pipe-dream or a denial of the truth. But while this apparently vain search goes on, that cross-fertilisation between biblical Christians in the established church and the free churches has been hindered and is in danger of lasting damage.

Without doubt, much more recent history has had a part to

play in the distrust that seems to have grown up between Anglican and non-Anglican Evangelicals. The well-publicised disagreement between John Stott and Dr Martyn Lloyd-Jones at an Evangelical Alliance sponsored meeting in the Westminster Central Hall undoubtedly opened a wound that has yet to be healed, though two decades have now elapsed. The rights and wrongs of this matter – what was said and what was not said – have been discussed before, save to say this, that the Roman Catholic question is an added dimension. The Nottingham Statement of 1977 says: 'Seeing ourselves and Roman Catholics as fellow Christians, we repent of attitudes that have seemed to deny it.' Only God knows who are his, and the posturing and extremes of some antagonists of Rome have been an affront to many. Nevertheless, unless those areas where Roman dogma are contrary to or in addition to the revealed word of God are addressed and repudiated, what fellowship can there be? If Evangelical Anglicans were to be identified with or party to unity with Rome, however distant in reality this may be, then a chasm would be opened up in Evangelicalism almost impossible to bridge. Unless we are agreed that the claims of Christ are exclusive as well as embracing, that 'no man comes to the Father but by me', that the gospel is the gospel of truth (Gal 2) and is the only way of salvation, then we are agreed on little and the common label of Evangelical that we share is but paper over the cracks of an unstable wall built on sand.

Much of the problem facing us today is due to lack of contact leading to suspicion and mistrust. Mistrust leads to fear, and fear to alienation. So many Evangelicals have become boxed in by shibboleths and bogeymen that do not bear examination. It is just not true that the individual Anglican ministers whom I know, love and trust are all leading to Rome. It is even preposterous to suggest it. Yet the published utterances and statements of some of their leaders have spread alarm. It is not true that Independent Evangelicals are only concerned with second-degree separation and the condemning of Evangelicals in the mixed denominations. It is not true that all charismatics are mindless and careless as to truth save that there be some common experience. It is not true that the Reformed churches are all cold and exclusive. Most of these fears and foibles are spread by the devil taking advantage of the lack of contact and trust among us.

True Evangelical unity is loving because God is love. It is love towards God so that we love what he loves. Love is not the reason for compromise, but a stimulus for sensitivity and care towards each other.

7

Para-Church Events and Evangelical Unity

Great strains have been put not only on Evangelical unity in general but the unity of the local church in particular by the mushrooming of 'extra-mural' activities in the wider church scene. These not only make considerable demands on the resources of the local fellowship but may even threaten its very life. Many a local church can thank God for the great city-wide evangelistic opportunity that has brought tangible and lasting fruit; yet many a local pastor has been driven to despair when his flock, having been introduced to the wider scene of celebrations, events, and national gatherings of various descriptions, return home seeking change – sometimes revolution – in the local fellowship. Evangelical unity can be strengthened and enriched by these events, but it can sometimes almost be damaged beyond repair.

Why this recent phenomenon? Para-church events have escalated in recent years with ease of travel and extended holidays. As has been said, these have greatly encouraged some local Evangelical churches. For some others it has been well-nigh disastrous. Not only have the resources of the local Evangelical church in time, money and personnel often been stretched, but the sophisticated, professional, exuberant

101

national events have often caused the home product to seem very ordinary, even second-rate, by comparison. Dissatisfaction with the local fare has been engendered among the people, which itself has caused bitterness and resentment in the pulpit. Yet it is quite clear that these national initiatives are not going to go away. They can either be ignored, be suffered under duress, or be used to further Evangelical unity. But if in the love of God that were to be, then there must be more mutual understanding, more cross-fertilisation than there is currently.

What demands does Evangelical unity make on the local church towards the para-church organisations and vice versa? It is obvious that a breed of Christians travelling from Spring Harvest via Greenbelt, Downs, Keswick, Royal Week, to Filey in Skegness to keep spiritually high, with booster jabs of celebration in between, brings no encouragement or profit to a local church. Quite the reverse. But surely I am exaggerating? Perhaps, but nevertheless I have met many such people. There is another possible exaggeration held by some that these events have nothing of value to contribute to the body of Christ. A carte-blanche rejection has left some churches vulnerable and damaged. It is my intention here to see if there is any middle way so that confidence between the local church and the central event can be built up. We will look at this matter under three headings: para-church events, para-church organisations, and united evangelistic missions.

Para-church events

For the length of this century and beyond, the annual preaching convention has been a part of the Evangelical scene. Frequently they are an occasion for a nationally-known preacher to minister over a few days within a local community. Sometimes, as at the Keswick convention in the past, these conferences were associated with a certain view of sanctification, or holiness, or the Lord's return, or revival, and so on. Because of this, some people viewed them as a threat to the emphasis of the local ministry. Such events have always faced a degree of suspicion and hostility, even though they are 'biblical' in content, devotional in application, and altogether honourable to the local fellowship in that they sought to build up rather than break down. How many missionaries first responded at Filey, and how many men were first called to the ministry at Keswick, eternity alone will record. Often these occasions were mountain-top experiences that have led to increased appetite for the word of God and service within the local church and beyond. Rather than undermining the role of the local church, they actually enhanced it. They were often occasions when the week-by-week, solid teaching ministry that had been received at home was applied to heart, mind and will, with the resulting decisions for service. The convention was the last link in the chain.

In my understanding, a new development began in Britain during the mid-50s and 60s, perhaps partly as a British spin-off from the Billy Graham crusades. British evangelistic associations were formed for city-wide evangelistic campaigns. This was hardly new, but certainly more frequent than previously. The Youth for Christ rally became a monthly event in many cities. I remember these well and with real affection. At a time when Christian young people were not encouraged to attend the entertainments of 'the world', when 'separation' was still a word that a Christian young person would understand, these evenings were somewhere to go, somewhere to meet friends where the atmosphere was freer, the music more accessible, and the preaching direct, relevant and challenging. God used these gatherings. If they were a threat to the local church, as a teenager I did not appreciate the fact, and, rather than being a hindrance to

Evangelical unity, they gave us the opportunity to meet Christians from other churches.

What about the situation today? It is much more complex, far wider reaching in its effect, potentially more dangerous to the local fellowship, and therefore a further strain on Evangelical unity. There is a plethora of inter-church happenings; it is getting out of hand. Of course, anyone has the right to call a conference; anyone with vision, drive and initiative can organise an event. This is a free country. Yet this important question must be asked: are the organisers of national events, city-wide initiatives, etc., mindful of where their supporters come from, their responsibility to them while they have them, and the situation to which they will return?

Some events, such as Downs and its sister conferences, are convened by a particular theological group to foster its emphasis and extend its influence. So be it. One can hardly be critical of that, even if one does not share their position. But what about events such as Spring Harvest where people come from wide-ranging backgrounds of churches and emphases? Now, let me state an interest at once. I have been privileged to be a speaker at Spring Harvest and am fully convinced of its relevance and theological sensitivity to a wide spectrum within biblical Christianity. I do not address myself to Spring Harvest in particular but rather to such events in general. Without doubt this type of event can make a real contribution to Evangelical unity, but there are potential dangers too. I make a plea for maturity and sensitivity on each side of the debate.

First, events such as Spring Harvest provide a marvellous teaching opportunity. The breadth of available experience and expertise over the whole gambit of subjects relevant to the Christian makes for a wonderfully constructive occasion in the life of the ordinary believer. He can digest, learn and subsequently apply what he has been taught.

Secondly, they are great occasions for praise. For many groups and individuals coming from small and isolated Christian communities, the opportunity to join with many thousands of like mind is a great joy. Much of the music, though not to my taste, is undoubtedly uplifting. The new songs composed by dedicated men are biblical, gloriously alive and undoubtedly used to uplift Christ in the hearts of those that love him.

Thirdly, these are times of cross-fertilisation. I have already referred to being interviewed on the house TV station at Spring Harvest when the first question revealed some surprise at my background and the supposed emphasis that I represented. I assured this questioner that I would never be elected as spokesman or delegate by any constituency, but that nevertheless I was not ashamed of the insights and emphasis that I believed God had given me. There can be no doubt that such occasions give opportunity for two-way bridges to be built, understandings to be received and shared, and confidences engendered.

Fourthly, they are wonderful occasions for young people. Here we touch on the tricky subject of gospel rock, etc. For me gospel rock is not, nor ever can be, God's primary method of evangelism. To my dying day I will be convinced that it is by the word shared and gossiped around the world that God in his grace saves some. I have seen it clearly demonstrated that it is yet 'by the foolishness of preaching' that God brings his own to himself. Yet I have come to a hesitant conclusion, which I will try to explain.

My children, being typical of their age, are keen on pop music. Without some degree of parental restraint it would be played from first thing in the morning to last thing at night – and longer, if that were possible. Many of today's pop groups are demonstrably influenced by the occult, perverted in lifestyle, and downright wicked in lyrics and in presentation. In short, they are of the devil. Therefore I have become glad that my children have come into contact with Christian bands and follow them with keen interest. Although I cannot relate to their music, I realise that they are young people of prayer, truly concerned that they should be used in the service of God.

So often we feel that 'take my voice and let me sing' must be in the accepted terms of a previous generation. Yet Bev Shea (God bless him) and others like him and the choirs of our youth have little appeal today. I have a suspicion that our parents bought the latest Bev Shea as a Christian substitute for the Bing Crosby type music of their day. Perhaps there is nothing new about today's situation. Whatever, I have come to believe firmly that my children are in safer hands with some of today's Christian groups than they are with their depraved, ungodly counterparts so prominent in today's entertainment scene. Events such as Spring Harvest are opportunities to meet, hear and enjoy the best of today's Christian musicians.

But there are dangers too, dangers of which I presume the organisers of national events are well aware. I plead with them now to be sensitive to the local church, for that is where their supporters have come from and to where they must certainly return.

First, a national conference to which Christians are drawn from local churches demands respect for the local church. To tell those assembled to leave their home church is a flagrant abuse of trust. It must never be allowed to happen. Rather, teaching must be given (as it often is) as to the way that the local pastor can be encouraged and the people of God enhanced by what has been both given and received.

Secondly, to counsel a man or woman contrary to the teaching he has received at home is again unethical. The first question at such a time is 'What does your pastor think?' and the last, 'Go and tell your pastor what has taken place.' But what if you think the local man is wrong? Before God you feel this person is crying out for something that his fellowship either cannot or will not give. The home church must still be respected. One can speak in terms of general principle, point out helpful books to read, and, best of all, relevant passages in Scripture. But one is still subject to the local church. There is no authority for freelance, unaccountable ministry apart from the body of Christ which is the church.

Thirdly, to give the impression, though unintentional, that the atmosphere and style of the conference should be the weekly norm back at home has led to much difficulty. I do not believe for a moment that mature leadership does give that impression, but there is clearly a danger. After the great congregation, the convention speaker and the wonderful praise, the home church can seem insignificant, ordinary hidebound by tradition and drab. Often the result is terrible dissatisfaction on the part of the returning people and deep resentment on the part of the home leadership. The whole point of a holiday is that the change of scene and diet prepares you for the coming demands of daily life. So it is with conferences. Certainly, the local church must be open to what the Spirit is saying. Certainly, the regular minister must be sensitive to the needs of the people. But there are other considerations too, the most obvious being that whereas the conference or convention addresses for a limited period people of comparatively like mind – else they would not be there – with all the best talent available, the local church ministers to a diversity of ages, backgrounds, likes and dislikes, week in and week out, often without the aid of talented musicians and singers. Old Mrs So-and-so on the organ certainly fades into insignificance by contrast.

A local pastor has a responsibility for the whole church, feels it his responsibility as much as he is able to minister to every need, and can only move as fast as is wise – and sometimes that can be painfully slow. I am not the only minister who has waited with mild amusement for the returning group to come to the vestry to say, 'What we need here Pastor, is....' And sometimes they are right! But sometimes the reply is, 'I agree with you, but you must wait for a while.' A true pastor loves all his sheep, and will not trade one group against another or feed the particular appetite of one to the starvation of another. He must try to cater for divergent tastes, differing fears, hopes and aspirations, encourage the backward, restrain the forward, and seek to minister the whole counsel of God. The leaders of national events can help the local pastor by seeking to explain this at their gatherings.

Let me say one or two things before closing this section. A pastor should try to trust his people – and himself. There is such a lack of confidence around today. While I was at Spring Harvest I met several people who said, 'Don't tell my pastor I am here.' How sad! What are the implications of such statements? One, that the local minister is so distrustful of the biblical foundation he has laid that he has no confidence that it will meet a test. Two, that the event to which the member has gone is about destroying foundations, when it is not. Three, that there is such a lack of love and confidence between pastor and people that the member has to creep away like a truant from school. I have really felt that I am getting somewhere when my own people, reporting back from some national event, have said, 'We could accept this but not that,' 'We felt that such was of God but we were hesitant about the other.' That shows growing maturity and discernment in the word of God. When one's young people can choose for themselves what is a balanced diet and, even better, show an ever greater appetite for home cooking, then all we can do is praise God.

One last plea to organisers of national events. When you choose a speaker, do not do so to use him for your own ends. 'To have him will represent that position, or give us kudos in that area' may be wise to the world but is hardly honouring in the kingdom of God. No one wants to be used. Rather, the question should be 'Is he the man for this hour? Is the Spirit of God on him for ministry to this situation?' There is only one aim, and that is the glory of God. Any other consideration is shallow by comparison.

Then there is the matter of united missions. I have in mind such events as Mission England and area-wide evangelistic initiatives. What a strain these can be on local Christian unity!

Quite recently at a minister's fraternal, a fellow minister, having given a sigh of relief that Mission England was over, then went on to speak of the latest 'event' to impinge upon him. Let me say straight away that two of my family came to know Christ at Mission England, and that almost every baptismal service since has included those who were brought to decision at that time. I remember Mission England with great joy. Nevertheless, there is a sense in which I know what my friend meant. Such happenings do bring their strains. And what has Evangelical unity to say to these things?

First, there is the whole question of 'mixed' evangelism. The principles that I have laid down in the biblical section must be brought to bear here. No one with any discernment can enter into a project like Mission England without much heart-searching. Is such a project a good investment of the time, money and energy of the local church? Will the fellowship be deflected from its primary task? Who will the evangelist be and can he be trusted to preach a full gospel? What form will the preliminaries take? Who will the counsellors be? How will enquirers be followed up? Where will they be placed? These are but a few of the questions to be asked by anyone who takes their responsibilities seriously.

I cannot speak of other areas, but in East Anglia South much care was taken which led to encouaragement from some and criticism from others. First, our chairman was a man of unequivocal Evangelical convictions. Secondly, every executive member acknowledged his agreement with the Lausanne Statement of Faith. Thirdly, we resisted at some pain Roman Catholic participation in counselling, follow-up and referral of enquiries. Fourthly, following on the exhaustive training programme, each application to be a counsellor was individually and carefully examined. Churches that wished to participate, over which there were queries, were investigated. Allocations of enquirers were unashamedly directed to participating churches where possible – those who had indicated their oneness with us in having trained personnel and counsellors. And God was very good to us! Of course, there were problems. Very few of us would want to do it again for some time. The demands on time and energy were overwhelming. Nevertheless, there has been lasting fruit. Real friendships have been formed, trust has increased between churches, and Evangelical unity has been furthered.

When I was asked to lead a united church mission recently, I tried to apply some of the lessons that had been learnt at East Anglia South. We set out with an agreed full statement of faith, in this case the old IVF statement, to which participating churches had to agree. Immediately several of the churches who had expressed an interest withdrew. Perhaps this was for the best, for how can one evangelise with those who do not know the evangel?

Evangelical unity demands certain things from those who participate in united evangelistic initiatives and those who do not. One is that we should be completely open and honest. Some of the propaganda distributed prior to Mission England, antagonistic to Billy Graham, was well-nigh libellous. I quote from one such publication:

> The greatest crisis point, however, as far as the effect of modernism on Graham's course is concerned, brought tremendous sadness to those who love the Gospel of truth. In response to a query regarding the content of Graham's preaching, W.H.

Martindale, Spiritual Counsellor at Graham's headquarters replied, 'Mr. Graham believes that we are saved through the blood of Christ, however this aspect of Christian doctrine he does not emphasise in his messages. This is the duty and prerogative of the pastors.' This statement goes unretracted and underlines the tragic weakness of the kind of message being preached. Any preaching which deliberately omits the atoning blood of Christ cannot be truly called evangelistic. The preaching of the blood lies at the very heart of truth of redemption. If no other evidence existed then this matter alone is sufficient to wipe out any possibility of association with Billy Graham Crusades.

Rather than omitting the atoning blood of Christ in his preaching, Billy Graham preached almost nothing else! Bible-believing Christians must never descend to the gutter, however deeply an issue is felt.

Another thing is that there must be mutual understanding and trust. Those who do not participate in inter-church missions from strongly-held convictions must believe that those who do participate feel constrained to do so from equally-felt convictions. And those who, after carefully weighing the issues in the balance, find the scales tipping towards participation must not feel either pity or scorn for those who did not. Many Christians sacrificed much by not being involved in Mission England, but their consciences were kept clear before God. Of course, they would love to welcome new born-again Christians as much as any church. But because of their understanding of the mind of Christ, they had to stand apart. We each have to give an account before God for our own actions, and we should leave the day of reckoning till then.

One last word to the organisers of such nation-wide events as Mission England, and one that is relevant to our subject of Evangelical unity. May I ask as humbly as I can, were you always as sensitive to others' consciences as you should have been? To put it mildly, when men of no known Evangelical persuasion are asked to be prominent at related promotional events, it makes life very difficult for those who have sought to support you. Were there not enough men of firm biblical conviction to make pointless the chasing after random famous names so as to give weight to the platform? Were you always as thoughtful and sensitive to us as we endeavoured to be to you?

Another different but related area is the whole matter of training for the ministry and Christian service. The matter of Evangelical unity addresses itself to the whole matter of Bible and theological colleges. When a man or woman hears the voice of God and requests or needs intensive residential teaching, the local church has a problem – not an unpleasant problem, but a problem all the same. Where should they be encouraged to apply?

We have some fine institutions of training in this country today. But the colleges must remember that they receive students on trust from the local fellowship. If they profess to be biblical and conservative in doctrine – then they must be faithful to that. If the local fellowship discovers that faith has been shaken and truth questioned, only grave distrust can ensue. Of course, some colleges that lecture for outside examination boards have to lay their students open to modern critical scholarship. Of course, some are affected by newly-discovered emphases and viewpoints. Nevertheless, Evangelical training colleges do have a responsibility to be what they profess to be. College days are a time for reflection and re-examination of what one has received and believed, and the sending church must understand that. It must also be assured that those into whose hands we have placed our members will be loving and supportive of them, and particularly mindful of the sending church. Trust has to be built up.

A little while ago, one of my members had disastrous results in her degree exams. In her dejection her immediate response was to apply to the first Bible College that came to mind, who accepted her by return of post. We were ignorant of her application until a cursory letter requesting a reference was received. It was explained that before our church supports applications for further training, there are exhaustive procedures to go through in the fellowship. Interviews must take place, much prayer made, the financial implications entered into, and the reason why God has prompted this course of training discovered. Of course, the matter came to nothing, and this delightful person is going on wonderfully with the Lord in her God-directed vocation. But the whole incident illustrates that unity demands that we engender trust between church and college, and that the churches themselves do more to be knowledgeable of and helpful towards the places of further Christian training that are doing such splendid service today.

Perhaps the area where unity is best demonstrated is with Evangelical missionary societies. These instruments of the love of God are still being used after decades of service. Of course, even the finest societies are not immune from the tensions we all face. The charismatic/non-charismatic debate, for instance, has touched everywhere. But nevertheless, within Evangelical missionary societies, Christians of various denominations and nationalities are brought under an agreed statement of faith for the primary purpose of proclaiming Christ to the lost. We have much to learn from them.

8

The Dangers of Sectarianism

What is a sect? A look at the Oxford Dictionary will help us.
In its religious usage (it has others) it means:
   (1)   'A religious following – adherence to a particular
         religious teacher or faith.' In this sense it can be
         applied to any of the world religions.
   (2)   'A system of belief or observance distinctive of one of
         the parties or schools into which the adherents of a
         religion are divided.' This is the definition which we
         will particularly note here. It is amplified as 'a system
         differing from what is deemed the orthodox tradi-
         tion; a heresy'. It is further defined as 'a body of per-
         sons who unite in holding certain views differing
         from those of others who are accounted to be of the
         same religion, sometimes applied to parties that are
         regarded as heretical, or at least as deviating from the
         general tradition'.
   (3)   Similar to the above is the usual modern use: 'A sepa-
         rately organised religious body, having a distinctive
         name and its own places of worship; a denomination.
         Also in a narrower sense, one of the bodies separated
         from the Church. It is applied to the various bodies of
         Dissenters by Anglicans, and to the whole of Protest-
         antism by Roman Catholics.' We would use it of those

> religious proselytising groups that are anti-Trinitarian and add to or subtract from the supremacy of Scripture.

Historically understood, it is quite a privilege to belong to a sect. The Clapham sect was a name of derision for that group of the early nineteenth century composed of men such as Wilberforce, Macaulay and Thornton, who realised that Evangelical conviction must lead to practical application in regard to the needs of society.

In a book called *Religious Sects* Bryan Wilson seeks to define the distinguishing marks of a sect in its modern sense. I will use some of his criteria to endeavour to mark out disquieting trends. Now, we know that a sect is anyone who does not agree with us! It is the word that comes readily to the tongue when we wish to dismiss something or someone. The complexity and emotiveness of the word is obvious. Yet I have become convinced that the recent trends towards distrust on the one hand and separation on the other reveal many of the marks of sectarianism. Of course, it is always the established that seek to designate another group as the sect. We are all a sect to someone. But note this quote from Wilson with particular care: 'Sects were regarded as opposed to the church, even though sectarians saw themselves as reformers or restorers of the faith itself.'

There you have it. Reformers and restorers. The very names taken by two of the main emphases to grow up in the last twenty-five years of Evangelicalism. Whatever we mean by being 'Reformed' or by the restoration movement, it is quite clear that one of their effects has been towards polarisation. Seeing that I am not ashamed to apply the label 'Reformed' to myself, this is addressed to me as much as anyone else. The mark of the sect, Wilson argues, is divergent belief, separation and rejection of authority. Now, what is 'church authority' and by whom is it exercised? There is no united opinion on that, except surely for true Evangelicals who find their authority in the holy, inspired word of God. But sadly, having said that does not mean that we are preserved from fragmentation. Quite the reverse – it is rampant among us.

Wilson comes up with these definitions of a sect:

(1) Sects are voluntary bodies and there is an element of choice in subscribing to the sect's tenets.

(2) There is a division implied in the word 'sect'. The votary must choose the sect, but choice is mutual – the sect receives or rejects the applicant.

(3) 'The sect has a strong sense of self-identity: who is admitted becomes "one of us".' Wilson argues that the 'us' is set over against all else.

(4) The sect sees itself as an élite.

> The sect is the sole possessor of true doctrine, of appropriate ritual and of warranted standards of rectitude in social behaviour, regards itself as a people set apart, making claim, if not always to absolutely exclusive salvation, at least to the fullest blessings.

(5) Sects are disposed to exclusivity.

> Membership takes precedence over all other secular allegiance. In separating from other groups, sects impugn their sanctity and their warranty: belonging to a particular sect implies distance from, and perhaps hostility to other sects and religious bodies.

(6) Sects practice the expulsion of the wayward.

> The sect is self-conscious and its formation and recruitment are deliberate and conscious processes. Thus it is also a body with a sense of its own integrity, and a recognition that the integrity might be impugned by the careless or insufficiently committed member. Hence the sect expels the unworthy.

(7) The sect imposes standards on the individual member. He must be committed. 'Self-control, conscience and conscientiousness are significant characteristics of sectarianism.'

(8) Although sects assert an alternative set of teachings, commandments and practices from the orthodox, this alternative is never a complete and total rejection of all elements in orthodox tradition – otherwise we should not recognise the sect as being such. It is essentially a set of different emphases, with some elements added and some omitted. To propound this alternative, the sect must espouse some other principle of authority than that which adheres in the orthodox tradition and claim superiority for it.... Whatever it is, the sect rejects the authorities of orthodox faith.[12]

Now, let me make one or two things clear. Bryan Wilson, writing in 1970, was not addressing himself to the modern Evangelical scene but religious sects in general – eastern as well as western. In the above list I have endeavoured to include without omission what he designates as distinguishing features of a sect. As we seek to apply the above, I am calling no one a sect, except as others would count me as a member of one because I am a 'dissenter' by background and conviction. Yet I do suggest that recent years have seen a rise of the sectarian spirit among us. That the Bible stands implacably opposed to that is quite clear, as we have already discovered. Seeing that all Christians of goodwill would agree that what we are witnessing is not in the purposes of God, then we must come to the only possible conclusion that the sectarian spirit is being used by the evil one for his own diabolical purposes.

I have no doubt that the points of definition made by Bryan Wilson have struck a few bells in many a mind, as indeed they should. We will go through them. My commentary below corresponds to my numbering of Wilson's points made above.

(1)   No one is suggesting pressure or manipulation in forcing anyone to join an Evangelical group as defined in

this book. There have been reports of concern regarding some fringe groups of charismatic communities, but I am in no position to comment on them.

(2) No comment, except that we would all seek to preserve membership to the redeemed, and I suppose that makes us all sectarian to Wilson.

(3) Is it not true that the 'one of us' mentality is rampant today? Of course, only the sovereign God really knows if another is a brother or sister in Christ. But we certainly have a duty to inquire and to ascertain as clearly as possible whether another is 'of the way'. Nevertheless, within the body of Christ exclusivity abounds. 'Is he of our constituency?' we ask of another. Unless a man sports certain prescribed labels, he is bound to be under suspicion. One who cannot be categorised is a very queer fish.

It makes for a very easy life to be totally in with the group, absolutely part of a particular emphasis. It is always good to know who your friends are. But none of this can be what Christ intended when he prayed that we should all be one. Would any of us be so arrogant as to imply that the Saviour prayed that everyone should be as I am? God forbid! 'I can tell that you are one of us' has been a frequent comment addressed to me at conferences. I have never enquired who 'us' are, but to be counted among them appears to be the final accolade, the mark of full acceptance. I both believe in, preach and have experienced post-conversion blessing by the Holy Spirit (quite startling blessing in fact) but, by a refusal to preach it as a norm in every Christian or to insist on certain essential evidence following, I doubt if the 'us' would count me as a fully paid-up member of their group. It probably counts me out of another as well!

And this is not just to implicate charismatic weakness for categorisation. The Reformed are equally affected by the class mentality. Not to be one of them, or at ease with them, or to be held in suspicion by them is a most disquieting experience. There have been occasions when I have never felt more lonely than at a Reformed conference where I had imagined I was a part. Much of the same could be said of denominational gatherings. 'Is he accredited?' I have heard asked of a fellow minister, as if that were the only required mark for the servant of God to fulfil his calling.

(4) Élitism, I suppose, is the most common criticism made of Evangelicals by other sections of Christianity. It is that quality which makes us most distasteful to many. That 'blessed assurance', that inflexible self-righteousness that emanates from us. Never a hint of doubt, never a sense of need, independent of modern scholarship, insular of spirit, rebutting all overtures from outside. Of course, the carte blanche embracingness of ecumenical activities has put us on our guard, but surely we have a responsibility for contact, friendship and debate towards those of other persuasions and emphases than our own? If we do not minister Christ to these groupings, then who will?

One of the greatest privileges of my ministry has been to make opportunity to talk to fellow ministers of the things that we hold to be vital for a full-orbed biblical ministry. There has been undoubted fruit from such contact. And is it not just possible that we, too, have some things to learn and receive? Did the Lord's command to take the gospel to every creature include Muslims, Buddhists, pagans, the ignorant, the careless and sinful, the needy, the complacent, etc., but not 'Christians' of other emphases than our own? How will they hear if they have not a preacher?

But if Evangelicalism tends toward élitism, what about élitism within biblical Christianity? The Bible calls it pride. It is rampant among us and a primary cause of the distrust and lack of fellowship that has grown up. There was a day when to be an Evangelical was to have trust and fellowship right across the various denominational groupings. 'All one in Christ Jesus' Keswick proudly and correctly bannered across its tent.

(5) 'Exclusive? Well, that is not true of us!' You may object to this statement. But just think a bit. Are you quite sure? Communion means by definition meeting with God and meeting with each other. But some will not allow born-again believers to take communion with them, in direct contradiction to the word of God. We should heed God's word concerning our attitudes: 'A man ought to examine himself before he eats of the bread and drinks of the cup' (1 Cor 11:28). Some have to produce a letter to convince a group that they are 'one of us'. None would say explicitly that it alone possesses the truth, but it would certainly imply this. A positive reply to the question 'Are you in a mixed denomination?' counts some out, despite the grace of God counting them in. 'What translation do you use?' is another test of orthodoxy – as if God had done something in 1611 which he had neither done before nor since. Are you only prepared to address the Almighty in Jacobean English in complete denial of the vision of the Reformers, who understood very well the working man's right to read God's word and humbly address his heavenly Father in language he could both use and understand? 'Did you take part in Mission England?'

Yes, and still thanking God for it. 'Are the gifts exercised in your fellowship?' And so one could go on *ad nauseam*. Whatever your reply to an ever-increasing list of pointed questions causes you to fall out with someone.

(6) Some of us have the painful responsibility of ministering to those going through all the guilt and withdrawal symptoms that come from leaving and forsaking their particular group. Were these people Moonies or Jehovah's Witnesses? I wish to God they had been – it might have been easier. They had come from groups which were very loving and supportive in many ways, but also very insular, possessive and authoritarian, and extremely directive in a variety of ways, both secular and spiritual. It had been discovered that there was only peace in the group when there was total conformity to its norms. Let the leadership be questioned, the authority of eldership be doubted, and see what happened. How sad! Paul says in 2 Corinthians 1:24 – 'Not that we lord it over your faith, but we work with you for your joy, because it is by faith you stand firm.'

David Prior comments on this in *The Suffering and the Glory*:

> Paul is determined not to dominate or manipulate. The word used for 'lording it' is the verb from the Greek noun for 'Lord' as applied uniquely and incontrovertibly to Jesus in the New Teatament – I believe over 400 times. It was the Greek form of 'imperator', the Latin title for the Roman emperor. Even more significantly, it is the Greek word used in the Septuagint (the Greek translation of the Old Testament) for Yahweh, the name of God as revealed to Moses at his commissioning. Paul is unambiguously telling the Corinthians: 'Jesus is Lord, your Lord, and I will do nothing to usurp

122

his pre-eminent place in your lives.' That is a searching
truth for any person entrusted with pastoral responsibility, because it is all too easy to take the place of Jesus in
someone's affections or allegiance.[13]

One of the marks of the true church is that it exercises
firm yet loving discipline. But no man dare take the
place of Christ in the life of another. The only ministry and control that a Christian leader has over
another is to point that one to Christ and lovingly
seek to apply the word of God to his situation. Then
why the horrid withdrawal symptoms experienced by
some in sections of the body of Christ when, for whatever reason, 'fellowship' is withdrawn?

I have become very troubled by a common practice
to which I have been party in the past – the refusal to
allow another to come to the Lord's table when under
church discipline. By whose authority is this, and on
what passage in Scripture is it based? If the table
shows forth the Lord's death, then the sinful Christian should be at the communion service to witness it.
If the hymn writer is correct in writing, 'No gospel
like this feast,' then that one should be under the gospel. If the communion is the place to 'examine oneself and so eat of the bread and drink of the wine',
then to forbid the wayward Christian to be present is
to deny him the God-prescribed opportunity. And if
that one continues to eat and drink in an unworthy
manner, then the responsibility and the inevitable
judgement is that one's alone.

I am very fearful of the rigid requirements
demanded by some for fellowship. The annual
renewal of membership vows and the requirement
for almost abject obedience to discipline may make
for a quiet life, but is it right? It also leads to over-

dependence, the inability to think for oneself, and the usurping of the individual's responsibility within the body. That it seems to work is not an adequate criterion, for it leaves damaged people behind.

Jesus said, 'Come to me, all you who are weary and burdened' (Mt 11:28). To those who come we have a responsibility, time-consuming and often heart-breaking though it be. And if we eventually discover that for any reason ours is neither the ethos nor the emphasis needed, than lovingly and carefully we must commend them to another, not just wash our hands of them and breathe a sigh of relief. How many times have I said in counselling, 'We are not the only Evangelical church in this town. We have not got the monopoly of the gospel. You will find several other fine churches in the area.' If we imply that no one comes to the Father except by us, then we are in serious difficulty.

(7) Self-control and conscientiousness are also marks of New Testament Christianity. Nevertheless, I am concerned about the restraints and requirements placed upon some Christians today. Rigid conformity, supervised tithing, regulated modes of dress, and prescribed attitudes seem to be growing characteristics in many circles. It is ironic that what was originally a heart-felt cry for freedom has left some more tightly bound than ever before. Similar characteristics are also seen in some of the ultra-separatist groups. There, too, only certain prescribed books are stocked and sold. 'Guarding the pulpit' often means only a select few are trusted to preach, and contact with other Christians is allowed less and less.

Of course, what all this reveals is lack of trust. If one feels that Dr Martyn Lloyd-Jones in his book *Joy Unspeakable* (Eastbourne, Kingsway, 1984) is likely to undermine in 250 pages all that has been ministered over years, then it is best not to stock Dr Martyn Lloyd-Jones. But do you distrust your own ministry that much? If a conference will expose my young people to such joy, life and experimental faith as to wreck in a stroke all that I have been trying to teach them, then common sense says I had better forbid them to go. But none of us has either the right or the authority to tell our people where they can or cannot go, what they can read or cannot read. Advise certainly – I do it all the time, but I do not claim to have the mind of Christ in everything. It is much better if, in the loving mercy of God, our people are made mature and discerning in Christ for themselves. How marvellous if they can say, 'I found this helpful but not that.' 'I did not get on with such a book because of this,' 'I enjoyed what I heard to a point but I could not accept the whole package,' or 'It has whetted my appetite for the regular ministry of the word.' When that happens, we know that our people are growing into Christian maturity.

We give our young children a very carefully controlled diet, but as they grow up they begin to feed themselves. It is a sad reflection on some ministers that their spiritual oversight gives their people so very little choice of food. Ours is the responsibility to lay down guidelines, to teach and instruct, but also to allow people to eat where they want from time to time. They will soon come home when they discover that the apparently tasty fare does not satisfy.

(8) Once again the danger signals are obvious and real. Authority is a buzz word among Evangelicals. What is it? On whom does it rest? How is it recognised? How is it exercised? 'Do you recognise our authority?' a young believer is asked.

Paul's letter to the Galatians is all about authority.

Paul establishes his rightful authority under Christ, yet his injunction to the members is clear and binding: 'It is for freedom that Christ has set us free. Stand firm, then, and do not let yourselves be burdened again by a yoke of slavery' (Gal 5:1). Woe betide us if we yoke our people by making them our slaves and burden them afresh when Christ has set them free.

In his very helpful book, David Prior draws out the nature of sectarianism in the church at Corinth to which Paul addressed himself in his second epistle. Although Paul was an apostle of the Lord, it is quite clear that his opponents criticised

▷ his behaviour – 'Our conscience testifies that we have conducted ourselves in the world, and especially in our relations with you, in the holiness and sincerity that are from God' (2 Cor 1:12)

▷ his decisions – 'When I planned this, did I do it lightly? Or do I make my plans in a worldly manner so that in the same breath I say, "Yes, yes" and "No, no"?' (2 Cor 1:17).

▷ his lifestyle – 'I beg you that when I come I may not have to be as bold as I expect to be towards some people who think that we live by the standards of this world' (2 Cor 10:2).

His whole ministry was brought under question by a super-spiritual group who said, 'Where is the evidence that God is really at work with him?' This is implied in 2 Corinthians 13:2–3 – 'I already gave you a warning when I was with you the second time. I now repeat it while absent: On my return I will not spare those who sinned earlier or any of the others, since you are demanding proof that Christ is speaking through me.'

126

Demanding a proof that Christ is speaking through a believer is the very essence of the sectarian spirit. Recently a close friend who took early retirement from a most prestigious career to go into the ministry was called upon by the leader of a new fellowship a few hundred yards down the road. Now, my friend is able and totally dedicated, with an absolutely Christ-centred and biblical ministry. But the work is hard, the encouragements few, and the set-backs numerous. In short, he is a man of God called to a most difficult situation. The elder from down the road (and why plant a church there, anyway, when vast areas of Britain are crying out for biblical ministry?) said, 'Why not join us? If the Lord was with you, you would have seen blessing. Our fellowship has increased in the last few months while you have hardly grown at all.' So tangible growth and influence is the infallible mark of the blessing of God? If that be so, then the whole of church history has to be rewritten. Explain that to Cranmer, Ridley and Latimer. Tell that to Bunyan in the woods or Jonathan Edwards when he was put out of his church in Northampton, Massachusetts. Explain that to the Saviour himself who found that 'there was no-one to help' (Is 63:5). If success per se and increased numbers on their own are the proof of Christ at work, then the Jehovah's Witnesses and Mormons must be right after all.

No, success has never been the infallible proof of the blessing of God, as Jesus clearly tells us:

> Not everyone who says to me, 'Lord, Lord,' will enter the kingdom of heaven, but only he who does the will of my Father who is in heaven. Many will say to me on that day, 'Lord, Lord, did we not prophesy in your name, and in your name drive out demons and perform many miracles?' Then I will tell them plainly, 'I never knew you. Away from me, you evildoers!' (Mt 7:21–23).

Here were confirmatory signs without doubt. Prophecy, deliverance ministry, miracles – the whole works in fact. There was clearly evidence of power in their work. But whose power and what work? We should rejoice in the blessing of God when we see it. There are plenty of bitter spirits about who seek to decry, tear down, and deny what the Lord has done. But success in itself is the proof of nothing. The above passage needs much careful pondering, much seeking the mind of Christ, lest, being caught up in the 'signs following', we should be caught away from Christ himself.

David Prior observes:

> At bottom, the reason for this concentration on success is self-justification: if we hive off from the existing Church, either organisationally or simply by keeping ourselves to ourselves, we must justify the action by the results – however much we believe and declare initially that the new departure or the accepted policy of our church is a matter of obedience to the Spirit of God, of the Word of God, or both.
>
> The quotation Paul gives from Jeremiah is pungent and challenging: 'Let him who boasts boast of the Lord.' The fuller context in Jeremiah is equally relevant: we are urged not to boast in our wisdom, might or riches. A modern paraphrase might well run: 'Do not boast about your monopoly of the truth, the size of your congregation, or the amount you give away to missionary work; boast in the Lord who practises steadfast love, justice and righteousness in the earth.' Those last three priorities are the ones God looks for in his Church.[14]

What about 2 Corinthians 10:10 – 'Some say, "His letters are weighty and forceful, but in person he is unimpressive and his speaking amounts to nothing"'? The opponents of Paul sought to dismiss both him and his ministry. 'Well, of course, he seems impressive by his writing, but that is an illusion, he is nothing really,' they said. The rejection of a man's ministry is the cardinal feature, the almost invariable tactic of the opponent of Evangelical unity. The decrying of others is the diabolical feature of this age. I suppose there is not a single ministry with which we would be in total agreement – except our own. So we ridicule or debase or deny what another man is doing for the Lord. But none of us is infallible. Poole-Connor comments:

> Infallibility has great attractions. To deliver ex cathedra decisions concerning doctrine and the will of God solves so many difficulties. An early follower of Mr. Darby, who came much under the sway of his impressive personality, later declared that during the period of his spiritual subserviency his Christian experience was of the pleasantest kind. It was all so simple, he said. To accept the will of God – that is, as revealed in Scripture – that is, as Mr. Darby interpreted it – what more delightful? 'My creed is the Bible' is a phrase that can often be misleading; what the speaker really means is 'My creed is the Bible as I interpret it'. Private interpretation of the Word must be a man's own guide, and his own responsibility; but he should not try to impose it on his brethren, or regard them as inferior if they cannot see it exactly as he does.[15]

Sometimes the rejection of others is sheer wickedness, stooping to lies and the gutter tactics of the world, which is totally unacceptable of followers of Christ. We have already seen some of the criticisms made about Billy Graham. He would not have my full support in every action or stance (he won't lose sleep about that), but to say of him, as does Malcolm H. Watts in the booklet *Mission England – Is It Scriptural?*, 'Dr Graham's "evangelistic message" does not spell out in any detail, or with any preciseness, the vital doctrines of the historic Christian Faith' will have to be accounted for.

None of us is wholly innocent in this regard. I remember going to hear David Watson with a negative spirit because of some stories I had been told regarding his involvement with Roman Catholics (I told him of my serious hesitations in this area to his face later on – it is better that way) and coming away confessing that rarely if ever had I heard the gospel so fully, so graciously, so simply explained to many who knew little of the Saviour – including Roman Catholics. I repeat, his position on the Catholic issue is not mine, but dare I dismiss one whom God has honoured? Well done, good and faithful servant. Again, the ministry of Dr Peter Masters, so stridently separatist, is at variance in some areas with my thinking. But that will hardly worry him. Yet God has used this man uniquely for the training and encouragement of pastors and preachers. Who can but rejoice that such a man with such a ministry is at work in the centre of the metropolis?

A friend of mine once said that 'one maggot spoils the whole salad', implying that if someone falls at one point then his whole ministry can be totally discredited. But that is wrong, terribly wrong. By that criterion my ministry is nothing and neither is anyone else's. Paul knew the truth. In 2 Corinthians 4:1–2 he says that it is only by God's mercy that any of us has a ministry, therefore we must renounce secret and shameful ways. We should note and remember verses 7–12 of that chapter – and what we remember for ourselves we should remember for others. We are not to condone wrong but seek to applaud that which is good.

I wonder who the 'super-apostles' of 2 Corinthians 12:11 were? Whoever they were, Paul, though hesitant to boast, says, 'I am not in the least inferior.' Great things were done among the Corinthians when he was with them. Dare we dismiss what God is doing for another, any more than we could condone his dismissal of us?

Of course, the very reaction to the 'super-apostle' has led some to glory in small things. Seeing very little tangible evidence of salvation and spiritual growth, they fool themselves that this was what was intended. Blessing, then, is by definition suspicious. People being saved must imply a cheap gospel. Large numbers gathering to hear the word of God preached must imply compromise somewhere. We have all met such thinking. But Paul's defence before the 'super-apostles' was that what they claimed he too had seen. Also, all that they said of themselves had been his experience too. The distinguishing feature had been not that there were no signs, wonders and miracles, because there were, but 'great perseverance'. The Corinthian church was not inferior to other churches.

I speak with great care. The judgemental spirit has been with us long enough. The same groups have made their views clear and have followed what they are convinced is the way of obedience sufficiently for us to ask, 'Is God especially with them?' What are the clear signs that they have the mind of Christ? Let us all be bold enough to ask ourselves the same painful questions, and come to the same painful conclusion. Let us heed Paul's injunction in 1 Corinthians 10:12 – 'If you think you are standing firm, be careful that you don't fall!' The result will be that we, being cast down before the Lord, seeking his mercy for our own shortcomings, will be hesitant to judge others when we are mindful of our own condition. Jesus himself warned:

> Do not judge, or you too will be judged. For in the same way you judge others, you will be judged, and with the measure you use, it will be measured to you.
>
> Why do you look at the speck of sawdust in your brother's eye and pay no attention to the plank in your own eye? How can you say to your brother, 'Let me take the speck out of your eye,' when all the time there is a plank in your own eye? You hypocrite, first take the plank out of your own eye, and then you will see clearly to remove the speck from your brother's eye (Mt 7: 1–5).

Many churches today are badly served by their leaders. Their people do not realise that the ones whom they trust, honour and support, rather than spending their time preaching the gospel and their energy feeding and pastoring the flock, are travelling great distances, spending much time, and using up their resources of mind and body to tear down what another has diligently raised up, repudiating the ministry of others and separating themselves from the body of Christ. Let the people themselves rise up and say to the wayward shepherds, 'Enough is enough.' Why bear it any longer? If a man seeks to isolate you from your brother, say no. If a man attacks another brother, tell him you will not tolerate it. If he preaches contrary to your certain knowledge and experience of the love of Christ, though he speak in terms of the highest orthodoxy, put him out. To do otherwise is wrong, as Paul said:

> For if someone comes to you and preaches a Jesus other than the Jesus we preached, or if you receive a different spirit from the one you received, or a different gospel from the one you accepted, you put up with it easily enough [to your shame].
>
> In fact, you even put up with anyone who enslaves you or exploits you or takes advantage of you or pushes himself forward or slaps you in the face [and that is madness] (2 Cor 11:4, 20).

We are all afraid of standing up for what is right. Sometimes a pastor must stand against his people; sometimes I am afraid it has to be the other way round. When a leader takes to himself what belongs to Christ, or, for reasons known only to him, seeks to break up the body of Christ, then he must be confronted. Undoubtedly this is a last resort. Such action would be humanly distasteful to anyone. But Scripture is plain:

> Have you been thinking all along that we have been defending ourselves to you? We have been speaking in the sight of God as those in Christ; and everything we do, dear friends, is for your strengthening. For I am afraid that when I come I may not find

132

you as I want you to be, and you may not find me as you want me to be. I fear that there may be quarrelling, jealousy, outbursts of anger, factions, slander, gossip, arrogance and disorder (2 Cor 12:19–20).

Those who perpetrate factions and disorder are troublers of the body of Christ and must be confronted. Here is the test: a pastor's authority should be used for building us up, not for tearing us down (2 Cor 13:10).

9

Misunderstandings

If trust is to be built up, misunderstandings recognised for what they are, prejudice – which is an ugly, ungodly thing – be cleansed away, then ignorance must be addressed by the gracious Spirit of God.

That the things of which I have been speaking still exist among us can be seen in this editorial published in the half-yearly prayer letter of a missionary society:

One of the most disquieting features of current evangelicalism throughout the western world is the abandonment of traditional services of worship and methods of evangelism. Services and methods which lie closer to the ever-growing entertainment pursuit than to Biblical principles have become common with many, with Gospel concerts and drama ousting the preaching and systematic teaching of God's truth. The 'evangelical sandwich' of hymns interspersed with Bible reading, prayer and preaching is heaped with ridicule and substituted with choruses and ditties, the impoverished content of which demands rhythmic tunes andmuch repetition. Clearly, this is zeal outrunning understanding and carnal energy being mistaken for spiritual power.

It is, moreover, a vote of no confidence in those methods God has blessed and used so abundantly in past days. Great hymns are at once the product of revival and have been much used in revival, while the public reading and preaching of the Scriptures are not only commanded, they have been powerful instruments in the great awakenings of the past. The Reformation itself was both inspired and fostered by the return to God's infallible word after centuries of departure into man-made errors. Subsequent history attests this to be, not a one-off event peculiar to the sixteenth century, rather a pattern which was repeated in following centuries.

Our allegiance must be to those 'old paths' though regretting that we cannot co-operate with those friends who believe new times demand new methods. We canot but adhere to those ways which God has been pleased to use in former days while continuing to pray that He will be pleased to use them again in our time.

This extract was printed by a society that I both love and trust, doing great work for the gospel. Nevertheless, it reveals all that leads to distrust and antipathy in Evangelicalism today. That it was written in good faith and firm conviction I know, because I know the one from whose pen it came. Certainly, each fresh movement of the Spirit has been 'inspired and fostered by the return to God's infallible word', and any new claim should be measured against that. But in every awakening God has done something new: the return to Scripture at the Reformation, its systematic exposition and application by the puritans, open-air preaching in the eighteenth century awakening, the start of the modern missionary movement with William Carey at the end of that century, the great gospel preaching under Spurgeon, Moody, etc., in the nineteenth century.

Hymn singing was unknown to the puritans and they would not have tolerated it. Hymnology was born in controversy and opposition. Each of the subsequent movements of God has provided its own hymnology for the praise and glory of God; new styles and format to speak to a new time and situation. We love the insights and treasure the vast heritage that the great hymn writers have left us. Yet to imply that everything they wrote was of lasting value would be as

senseless as saying that everything today is 'choruses and ditties, the impoverished content of which demands rhythmic
tunes and much repetition'. No doubt the same was said of
that which has now become precious among us and venerable
with age.

It would be very sad if God had nothing to say to us for our
time, nothing to strike a chord in the ears, minds and hearts
of this generation. How sad if we should be the only century
of which future historians said there was nothing of immediate musical relevance to the age. The gospel is unchanging,
God's primary purposes and methods are unchanged. But to
insist that the only suitable language for worship is Jacobean,
the only suitable verses to sing are Restoration, the only suitable music to which to sing them Georgian, is to deny the
immediacy of our God and the relevance of the gospel message for today. God has raised up preachers for today – the
man who wrote the above is one of them – so why not Christ-
honouring hymn writers and composers too? They are so evidently among us.

This article entitled 'Separation – The Need of the Hour',
appeared in *Grace Magazine* (August-September 1985):

When we turn our attention to error we are often just as lax.
Activities associated with Billy Graham and Mission England
are again consuming the energy and attention of many, including Roman Catholics judging by the number of Billy Graham
posters now on display outside Catholic buildings.

Similarly the Ecumenical movement with its watering down
of the gospel and its reduction of Biblical truth to a mere insight
is to be separated from not associated with. Its close relative –
the charismatic movement – presents us with similar problems.
Ecumenism flourishes in a charismatic environment. Scripture
is relegated as present-day prophecies and direct communications from the Lord receive greater prominence. Is this really
the great work of the Holy Spirit we long for and pray for? There
is too much hard evidence of infiltration of churches and under-

mining of ministries by those who want a *Restoration* of what they believe are New Testament gifts of the Spirit and apostolic authority structures, for me to believe this is that great work of the Spirit. Is fellowship possible with those who engage in such things?

Did the writer enquire if what he concluded was altogether true before he went into print? Do we who stand for truth not also feel that we have a responsibility to the truth? No doubt what was written pleased some and confirmed others in their views, but was it true? Does not Christian love demand that enquiries are made? Judging by posters is perhaps not enough. And if what he says is true, is it true in every case? For quite clearly it was not, as I can testify after much pain and almost literal tears in writing to Roman Catholics explaining why they could not be used as counsellors in Mission England, and to their churches explaining why they would not be sent referrals from the follow-up team.

Again, the writer describes the charismatic movement as a 'close relative' to the ecumenical movement. 'Quite right,' say some; 'Tell the truth even when it hurts,' say others. He pleased a constituency, no doubt, and we all have a tendency to do that. But again, is what the writer says really true? Certainly he expresses widely-held fears, and certainly there are instances of what he describes, but is it true in its basic premise and sweeping conclusion? The Restoration movement would probably be highly amused at being linked with the ecumenical movement; many, rather than becoming ecumenical, have become extremely isolationist. Is it really true that among those who testify to a charismatic experience 'Scripture is relegated as present-day prophecies and direct communications from the Lord receive greater prominence'? If we share many of the writer's concerns, surely we should be careful, balanced and scrupulously honest in our writing?

Another example comes from much closer to home. Last year I had the great privilege of preaching at a convention sponsored by an English evangelist almost uniquely honoured by God for his straight, powerful proclamation of the gospel. No doubt to assure people that this convention was not 'charismatic' in the popular misunderstanding of the word, it was advertised as 'non emotional'. The implication is that charismatic worship is emotional (which it invariably is) and that non-charismatic worship is not (when it should be). If we are not emotional about the love of God and the cost to make a sinner whole, we will never be emotional about anything. This issue clearly revealed the problem that we face and the ever-widening gulf that is pushing Evangelicals apart and deepening mistrust among us.

Why do some feel so able to pontificate on the truth to the detriment of others? Because they have the teaching of the Bible on the matter. All right, so why do some, convinced that their stand is right, so attack those who differ yet who stand on the same biblical criteria and application of them? What about those who 'apply the regulation principle' yet come to a different conclusion? Common sense expects a little hesitancy, but Christian charity demands it. 'Well,' comes the reply, 'the Lord Jesus was quick to attack error, and unflinching in his attack on wrong. Paul could say to Elymas, "You are a child of the devil and an enemy of everything that is right!" So we must face error in such a way.' Are you sure? And what about those who differ not on some foundational truth but in its working out in fellowship and association? E.J. Poole-Connor observes:

> It has been suggested that both our Lord and the Apostle Paul used strong language in addressing enemies of the truth (Matthew xxiii, 33; Acts xiii, 9–10), and that therefore their followers may do the same. But the One was the infallible Judge, Who 'knew what was in man', and the other was speaking under

the direct inspiration of the Holy Spirit. Can the ordinary believer lay claim to such qualifications? The rule for the 'servant of the Lord' is that he 'must not strive, but be gentle to all, apt to teach; in meekness correcting them that oppose themselves; if peradventure God may give them repentance unto the knowledge of the truth.' (2 Timothy ii, 24–25).[16]

Love is not greater than truth, but a man who holds the truth will most certainly hold it in love (1 Cor 13:6). Love always rejoices in the truth. Love demands that we hold to and proclaim the whole counsel of God. And because God is love, then truth and love cannot be in contradiction. Some imply that it must be either one or the other, but the cross of Christ denies that – 'Oh trysting place [an appointed meeting place] where heaven's love and heaven's justice meet,' says the hymn writer. Why, then, have I felt more threatened and lonely in the company of those who hold in almost every respect the same truths as I?

Truth is not at the expense of love. If it is, something has gone wrong somewhere. But similarly, love is not at the expense of truth. Bland, all-embracing togetherness, pleasant, unpressured and undemanding, is not New Testament Christianity either. Error is an affront to God, the denial of his Son in his person and work a blasphemy, carelessness in studying and proclaiming the word of truth unforgivable. It is the truth that makes free, not love. So how can all these paradoxes be brought together?

If a man says to his wife, 'I love you,' she has the right to say, 'Show me.' Neither Christian love nor Evangelical unity has the right to declare as secondary that which is essential, or, for some temporary advantage, ignore truth in the name of love. For a husband to say, 'I love you', with no intention of seeking his wife's legitimate well-being is not love. Love is more than words and platitudes. As Christ said:

If you love me, you will obey what I command.... Whoever has my commands and obeys them, he is the one who loves me. He who loves me will be loved by my Father, and I too will love him and show myself to him.... If anyone loves me, he will obey my teaching. My Father will love him, and we will come to him and make our home with him. He who does not love me will not obey my teaching. These words you hear are not my own; they belong to the Father who sent me (Jn 14:15, 21, 23–24).

Yet the same wife we have referred to above will also say to her husband, 'If you love me you will love whom I love. You may not understand my family but they are precious to me and you will have to try.' Some within a family can be very difficult, and building up a relationship with them takes years of effort, but the effort must be made.

In the frightening denunciation of the scribes and Pharisees in Matthew 23, the Lord never questions whether they have grasped the letter of the matter. He does not grumble at their theology, but stridently attacks their self-righteousness: 'You blind guides! You strain out a gnat but swallow a camel' (Mt 23:24). Their crime was their failure to seek God in understanding the spirit of the matter. And what about us when we construct arguments on false premises and state them without acknowledging the exception? When we seek to feed and foster the fears of godly, sincere folk by exaggeration, pandering to their concerns and falling silent when the facts contradict the treasured thesis? There is no doubt that when the teachers of the law and the Pharisees brought the woman caught in adultery to Jesus, they had the authority and security of an accurate rendering of the text on the matter (Jn 8:5). But the bare text was not enough. There were other considerations. 'If any one of you is without sin,' said Jesus, 'let him be the first to throw a stone at her' (Jn 8:7). Even when we have correctly established what Scripture says, there will be a degree of hesitancy before the stone-throwing begins.

One of the sadnesses of the day is that in taking pot-shots at the enemy from behind our embattled positions, we are shooting at our own side. If we had heard what others had been trying to say, and stopped first for a moment to listen, then things may have turned out differently. Who is the enemy? Apparently the major struggle is not against 'the rulers, against the authorities, against the powers of this dark world and against the spiritual forces of evil in the heavenly realms' (Eph 6:12), but rather against the 'flesh and blood' of our brothers and sisters in Christ, who in honesty to God take a different position from our own. If only we spent as much energy in fighting the true enemy as we do each other. The devil must laugh when we shoot ourselves in the foot.

So let the distortions be faced for what they are. We are all subject to them, but none of us must knowingly perpetrate them. All traditional worship is not dead. The hymn sandwich may have no biblical authority, but in many situations God honours it as a framework for worship, reading of the word, and expository preaching. Whatever some say, there are great signs of hope and encouragement outside the specifically charismatic sector. The group which *Grace Magazine* serves, from which I have quoted negatively, nevertheless tells of new churches being planted, churches struggling and without leaders calling pastors, young men being trained to preach the word of life, men and women being born again of the Spirit, and congregations growing in several areas. To describe Grace Baptist Churches as dead, as some do, is a downright lie. How I shudder when some narrow-minded person wipes out whole areas of the church as dead. There are so many wicked distortions being promoted and circulated by those who should know better.

But for those mentioned above to say that 'seeing God is with us he is not with you' is equally untenable. The Jack Horner of nursery rhyme fame who put in his thumb and pulled out a plum and said, 'What a good boy am I!' was made to sit in a corner. And that is where most self-congratulatory people are. To be forced into a corner is to be in retreat, to be on the defensive, to have a very limited view of things. God is at work elsewhere. He is doing great things which should make us glad. He does not restrict himself to any one constituency, so that none should be proud and none dejected. To dismiss charismatics with a word, or even a booklet, will not deter the sovereign Lord from working where and with whom he will.

10

Where Do We Go from Here?

So then, what is to be done? Let me recap for a moment. This book is not about compromise; it is a plea that we should hold our distinctives in love. It is addressed to people of conviction, to those who are where they are because they believe themselves to be obedient to the word and led by the Spirit. Yet who, because they are honourable people, do not desire to build on the sand of misunderstanding, or to further their cause by feeding the fears of the misinformed.

Here is the moot question, and it has no easy answer. How does the equally sincere brother, following the same criteria as us, find himself in another place, sincerely holding another position? He is sincerely wrong comes the reply. Perhaps, but how can one be sure? From the Scriptures. But he too has the Scriptures.

One of the characteristics of the present time is the number of people who have changed their theological position in the last fifteen years. Previously they were men of the word, and still are. Both then and now they claim the leading of the Spirit. But they have changed not only by growth in grace but in doctrine and outlook. Some have found great comfort and strength in the doctrinal system sometimes called Calvinistic or Reformed. They have found tremendous confidence in the 'doctrines of grace', giving them a place of quiet rest where they trust in the eternal purposes of God. For many of my generation and older, discovering with the mind and heart the certainties of the faith was like starting all over again. The sovereignty of God is my only reason and hope for staying in the ministry.

Very many, perhaps the majority, of these same people have moved from their previous eschatological convictions. Some have moved from a 'closed' communion table to an open, and some by conviction have gone the opposite way. There are now charismatic Reformed conferences for ministers who perhaps five years ago would have been vehemently opposed to them. Many of the leaders of Restoration churches were elders in Brethren assemblies, and so we could go on.

It is not that what is true today may not be true of tomorrow. That could not be, but rather what is true of me today may not be true of me tomorrow. And if that horrifies you, think for a moment. In the late 60s I read *The Forgotten Spurgeon* by Ian Murray. It changed my life. But what if I read another such book? Again, I read *The Momentous Event* by Grier and it was a revelation to me. Perhaps there is another monumental book around the corner.

For me this matter is best illustrated by a conference for revival with which I have been involved as a committee member for many years. In the early 70s this was a large conference, drawing in equal proportions ministers and people from inside and outside the Baptist Union, with ministry from acknowledged Evangelical leaders from denominational as well as independent churches. Since then the committee to which I was first elected has undergone dramatic change. Though each person has believed himself faithful to his understanding of the leading of the Spirit, they are now ministering in vastly different areas of theological emphasis. Hardly any would stand quite where he did in the early 70s. As for the conference, more and more have found their needs met in gatherings that cater for their particular persuasion, whether it be charismatic, Reformed or denominational. The point I am making is that entrenched positions can make one blind to the word of God, deaf to the prompting of the Holy Spirit, and, worst of all, make one believe with Elijah that 'I am the only one left' (1 Kings 19:10), that I alone have the truth. Entrenched positions on secondary issues are dangerous and have been a greater hindrance to unity than almost anything else.

I have been led to the conviction that if someone is closed to the possibility of any fresh experience of Christ by the Spirit, or to any new truth being applied or clarified from God's unchanging word, then he is too closed. And if I confess that God has changed my insight, understanding and experience in the not-too-distant past, why should he not do so again? After all, God is quite at liberty to do so. It would be a pity if some, wishing to retreat or indeed advance from their present position, discovered that they had burnt every bridge behind them and made any possible readjustment impossible. Within the revealed absolutes there is flexibility apart from the fundamentals. Bible Christians have always differed. None of us is infallible. It is essential to look, listen and ponder before you declare something as being not of God.

As for me, I will quietly try to listen, constantly take what I see and hear to the word of God, discuss and pray it through with those I love and trust, and wait and see. If the matter passes the test of Scripture as generally understood by spiritual men under the authority of the word of God, then I will fearlessly address myself to it. If not, then I will say something like this: 'I do not understand or see the matter as you do, it is not according to my taste or personality, it is no help to me in my walk with Christ. Nevertheless, I love you, my brother, I am open to your insight, I am anxious to hear what the Lord is doing through you, I rejoice that God has been so generous in his dealings with you in love.'

Am I to let go of my most firmly held insights for the sake of Christian unity? Does love demand that I squash my emotions for the good of the whole? Certainly not! But love is needed in handling our convictions, sharing them, and addressing ourselves to those who differ from us. We are not at liberty to tamper with or in any way dilute God's revealed truth, but how we express ourselves will probably reflect how much we have of the mind of Christ. This was the testimony of those who knew the Saviour and heard him address his hearers: 'All spoke well of him and were amazed at the gracious words that came from his lips' (Lk 4:22); 'No-one ever spoke the way this man does' (Jn 7:46); 'Lord, to whom shall we go? You have the words of eternal life' (Jn 6:68). And Isaiah was given this prophecy concerning him who was to come: 'Nor was any deceit in his mouth' (Is 53:9). If only the same could be said for some of the 'spokesmen' of today.

Perhaps the most upsetting development of the last few years has been the tendency towards a perfectionist ecclesiology in Reformed circles. Seeing that the search is by definition impossible, should it even be attempted? The whole emphasis of this book has been the need for honesty before God and obedience to his word, so the answer should be yes. But who is even worthy of the effort, let alone having any hope of success? As individuals we are each responsible before God for our walk in obedience, and nothing but our best is good enough in the service of the King. Because his perfect purposes will only be realised at the second coming is no excuse for the tawdry and second-rate now. We have to try to be holy by the Spirit's help because he has commanded it, and that is sufficient for us.

Nevertheless, those in positions of leadership have a particular responsibility to minister the whole counsel of God. How can we willingly condone what is wrong or associate with what is clearly contrary to the revealed purposes of

148

God? As I look around me, there is so much that is not as it should be. And when I look to myself, my ministry and the church of which I am pastor, I see that this applies here too. To have fellowship in any local church is to be with some who have cardinal doubt, some who have fallen into obvious sin, some who have compromised the faith, many who are nothing like what God intended them to be. So should I withdraw from them? No, for such am I, and I would resent them withdrawing from me. In fact, the majority of our congregation seek God's face, have an amazing appetite for his word, show real marks of grace, and tangible signs of growth in holiness. So we go on together. And what is true of any local fellowship must also be true of a fellowship of churches. Were it not so, then the whole plan and purpose of Christ for his body is denied and frustrated. We were never meant to be single units in isolation from the whole. Dare we be less embracing than the grace of God?

Church history offers us a most salient lesson. E.J. Poole-Connor, writing of the 1859 revival in Ireland, tells of the catholicity of the Holy Spirit's operation:

> These facts are deeply instructive, and if (as there can be no doubt they do) they reveal the will of God, they show that in many matters on which we are accustomed to lay stress, His ways are not our ways nor His thoughts our thoughts. Neither sectarian division, nor the principle of 'going without the camp', received the least shadow of endorsement during the Ulster Revival. God wrought as impartially through the 'traditional churches' as He did through the Brethren assemblies; and the human distinctions between Anglican and Dissenter, Presbyterian and Independent, Baptist and Paedo-Baptist, seemed in that great day of visitation, to be as little more than the pre-occupation of children.[17]

For those who have separated recently, not over the preaching of error or a dilution of the gospel or rejection of particular truth, but because a God-honoured, Spirit-filled servant of Christ, but from a mixed denomination, has preached on an Independent platform, it must be asked, 'What has been achieved? Why are you more sensitive than those who have gone before you?' Was the speaker compromised, outside of the will of God, deaf to his truth? I think not. Clearly no new precedent has been set. All that has been achieved is desperate heartache for your leaders, great confusion to the people, further polarisation in the body of Christ. I repeat, what has been achieved? What profit has there been?

The day is coming, perhaps soon, when all this dissension and declension will seem at best trivial and at worst downright wicked. Before the end, when the forces of darkness will meet head-on with the forces of light, when tribulation comes, as it most surely will, then these things will seem like a gnat-bite to an elephant. The command is to 'be faithful, even to the point of death, and I will give you the crown of life' (Rev 2:10). For the great multitude who come out of the tribulation, their churchmanship and affiliations – or lack of them – will be nothing. What matters is whether 'they have washed their robes and made them white in the blood of the Lamb' (Rev 7:14).

And what of the charismatic groups, for whom I thank God in many ways? In the next room to me at Bible college (in 1965) was a godly but very noisy young man who, I was told, was charismatic. It was the first time I had heard the word used in its modern sense. But that was a long time ago, and much has happened since then. But what about our nation, and our world? Is there really any cause for triumphalism, any cause for satisfaction regarding the kingdom of our God and his Christ? Now that the charismatic movement itself is dividing, and dividing alarmingly, how much is that movement a demonstration of 'the work of one and the same Spirit' (1 Cor 12:11)? No one has been led into division by the one Holy Spirit, or into conflicting views by the Spirit of truth. As with the rest of Evangelical Christianity, something has gone wrong somewhere.

Perhaps the greatest step towards Evangelical unity would be to recognise that some of our differences are irreconcilable (baptism, for instance). Professor MacLeod (*Evangel* August 1985) says, and I tend to agree, though from a different standpoint:

> There is no hope of the dispute being resolved. Anglicans and Presbyterians may as well recognise that 'you shall have Baptists with you always'. Nor is it possible to gather the two views into one church. If only the mode were in dispute, union might be possible, provided paedo-baptists were prepared to accept immersion for the sake of the peace (whether they would have a right to sacrifice their freedom in this way is a moot point). But the prevalence of two views as to who should be baptised makes organic union impossible. However flexible paedo-baptists might be with regard to immersion, they could not abandon the practice of infant baptism, which they regard as a divine institution. So long as the differences remain, the existence of separate evangelical churches side by side will be a painful and humiliating necessity.

And so we could go on. The Calvinist/Arminian debate, or the Reformed/non-Reformed issue, are not just matters of emphasis. They are not, as some imply, just a matter of putting the stress in different places so that a little accommodation all round will solve the matter. They are emphases which touch on almost every aspect of Christian life – its doctrine and its practice. They affect how the gospel is preached, how the 'net' is drawn in, and what methods are appropriate. The two systems cannot be reconciled at a stroke.

The charismatic/non-charismatic situation has little or nothing to do with singing Scripture songs, raising one's hands in worship, and unstructured services. It is whether a post-conversion experience of the Holy Spirit, whatever you call it, is mandatory for every born-again believer or not, whether the baptism in the Spirit speaks of regeneration or not, whether the 'gifts' are to be exercised now or ceased with the completion of the written word of God. More than good will is necessary to harmonise these viewpoints.

Neither will the tension between Evangelicals in the mixed denominations and those outside be dealt with at a stroke. The mutual recriminations of compromise and perfectionism will still be made, though both are probably inaccurate and unjust. But certain things can and must be done. The Bedford Document, taken from a most helpful booklet *A Basis for Christian Unity* published by Bedford Evangelical Church – is certainly worth looking at in terms of enhanced association between Evangelicals:

(1) Preamble
  (i) This federation of evangelical churches will be limited to a defined geographical area (insert the name) so as to preserve practical fellowship among the churches.
  (ii) It is expected that some churches in this federation will have formal links with an association or denomination of churches, which are either exclusively evangelical or of a mixed character.
  (iii) The execution of some of the aims of this federation will not be easy and it is therefore expected that a particular church may better act in concert with some churches rather than with others.
(2) Membership
All churches who belong to this federation will be bound by the following conditions:
  (i) The wholehearted acceptance of evangelical beliefs as summarised in the doctrinal basis of the British Evangelical Council.
  (ii) The recognition of all who trust in Christ alone for salvation as members of the body of Christ and that the local church

is the visible expression of that body. Furthermore that such evangelical churches possess three essential marks, namely the preaching of the Scriptures, the administration of the sacraments – baptism and the Lord's Supper – and the exercise of discipline.

(iii) The intention in principle and practice to seek a Scriptural expression of visible unity, among all evangelical churches, which implies a process of continuous reformation of the church by the Word of God.

(iv) The approval of a formal federation of all evangelical churches as a means to achieve this unity, so far as such a federation encourages each church to confess without wavering all God's truth known to her and therefore involves no sacrifice of principle or testimony.

(3) Aims

(i) To share information so that the churches can pray for each other.

(ii) To confer on matters of common concern:
    (a) The definition of doctrine.
    (b) The exercise of discipline.
    (c) The fulfilment of our Saviour's great evangelistic commission.
    (d) The training of elders.

(iii) To meet for mutual fellowship, especially for the elders of churches.

(4) Business

(i) The nature, time, and place of meetings which shall be held under the auspices of this federation shall be determined by consultation between the elders of each church.

(ii) In order to facilitate the activities of this federation a chairman and secretary shall be appointed by the elders of the churches from among their own number and by mutual agreement. The appointment shall be for a fixed period of time.

(iii) Churches shall join the federation by the mutual consent of the member churches, and can be excluded from its fellowship, if the member churches mutually agree that a church has failed to fulfil any of the four conditions for membership.

The work of the Evangelical Alliance and British Evangelical Council must be seen as important and complementary. The Evangelical Alliance, which has recently restated its unequivocal stand on biblical truth, is making wonderful progress in putting the Christian viewpoint to the secular media, sponsoring national prayer, fostering understanding, and drawing together Bible Christians from a wide area and constituency. The British Evangelical Council, by conference and debate, is bravely and painfully meeting the issues described in this book, and is to be more than commended.

Certainly, the last thing that is needed is some new organisation to sponsor Evangelical unity. That in itself would be divisive and serve only to compound the problem. Professor Donald MacLeod again puts it succinctly:

> The important thing now is that Christians who bear the marks (not perfectly, but authentically) should recognise, love and serve one another; and that churches which bear the marks (again, not perfectly, but authentically) should, whenever possible, unite; and even where that is not possible, 'stand together, contending with one mind for the faith of the gospel.'

Note this verse by James Montgomery on the Moravian church:

> They walked with God in peace and love,
> But failed with one another.
> While sternly for the Faith they strove,
> Brother fell out with brother.
> But He in whom they put their trust,
> Who knew their frames that they were dust,
> Pitied and healed their weakness.[18]

The first four lines are a comment on modern conservative Evangelicalism. May the last three, by the grace of God, be our testimony to that grace at work among us by his Spirit.

Without doubt our greatest need is a fresh outpouring of the Spirit of God. 'Where the Spirit of God has full control sectarian barriers disappear, as the dry patches that divide pool from pool on the shore are swamped by the rising tide.'

Notes

1. Roy Coad, *A History of the Brethren Movement* (Exeter, Paternoster, 1976), pp. 116–117.

2. E.J. Poole-Connor, *Evangelical Unity* (FIEC), p. 13.

3. Handley Moule, *The High Priestly Prayer* (London, Religious Tract Society, 1907).

4. E.J. Poole-Connor, *Evangelical Unity* (FIEC), p. 191.

5. *Ibid.*, p. 192.

6. *Ibid.*, p. 200.

7. John Stott, *The Epistles of John* (Leicester, Inter-Varsity Press, 1964) (Tyndale Commentaries), p. 105.

8. Peter Masters, *Separation and Obedience* (supplement to *The Sword and the Trowel*, 1983) p. 6.

9. Geoffrey B. Wilson, *Corinthians II: A Digest of Reformed Comment* (Edinburgh, Banner of Truth, 1979), pp. 87–88.

10. Handley Moule, *The High Priestly Prayer*.

11. Dr Peter Masters, *Separation and Obedience*, pp. 9–11.

12. Bryan Wilson, *Religious Sects* (London, World University Library, 1970), pp. 26–27.

13. David Prior, *The Suffering and the Glory* (London, Hodder and Stoughton, 1985), pp. 46–47.

14. *Ibid.*, p. 182.

15. E.J. Poole-Connor, *Evangelical Unity*, p. 77.

16. *Ibid.*, p. 35.
17. *Ibid.*, p. 77.
18. E.J. Poole-Connor, *Evangelical Unity*.

Father, Make Us One

by Floyd McClung

Shortly before he died Jesus prayed for Christians today:
'May they be brought to complete unity to let the world know that you sent me . . .'

Christians do not believe all the same things. We do not see eye to eye on all matters. We find some people difficult to understand, difficult to *love*.

So can there be unity?

Floyd McClung offers his answer to that question. He knows the score—it isn't easy. We need to be realistic. Whether it's between individual believers or between whole churches, there is no easy way to unity.

But Christ prayed for it, so it has to be our priority. Unity of the Spirit now—unity of the faith to come. Self-denying love now—triumph over every hurt and misunderstanding a promise for the future.

How much do we want what Jesus wants?

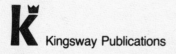 Kingsway Publications

Spiritual Gifts for Today?

by Herbert Carson

Some say that spiritual gifts and the ministries of apostle and prophet were withdrawn from the church at the time when the New Testament was written.

Others say that spiritual gifts have always been available to Christians, and any gift can be claimed by any believer at any time.

This book challenges both views. Carefully and methodically Herbert Carson sifts the biblical evidence, in the attempt to encourage both sides of the debate to align themselves with the Spirit of all truth, the One who both inspired Scripture and enlightens the hearts of believers today.

HERBERT CARSON'S writing and preaching ministry have been appreciated by thousands over many years. Since 1972 he has been Minister of Knighton Evangelical Free Church in Leicester.

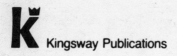

Kingsway Publications